Windsurfing

WINDSURFING

STEP BY STEP TO SUCCESS

ROB REICHENFELD

The Crowood Press

First published in 1991 by
The Crowood Press Ltd
Ramsbury, Marlborough
Wiltshire SN8 2HR

British Library Cataloguing in Publication Data

Reichenfeld, Rob
 Windsurfing.
 1. Step by Step to Success
 I. Title
 797.33

ISBN 1 85223 633 7

Note
Windsurfing is an international sport and different units of measure are used in various
countries. Sails are measured in square metres in most, but since Hawaii is the proving
ground for board design, feet and inches are used to descrive board size (with metric
equivalents in brackets).

Picture credits
All photographs by Rob Reichenfeld, except those on page 21 by
Anna-Marie Breuchert and pages 140–1, 143 and 147 (bottom right)
by Erik Beale.

Typeset by Keyboard Services, Luton, Beds
Printed and bound by Times Publishing Group, Singapore

Contents

Acknowledgements

This book was not a solitary project and I would like to thank everybody who so kindly gave of their time and knowledge, the following in particular:

Anna-Marie Bruechert, who endured my first drafts and helped enormously with writing the book.

Ian Boyd and Christine Spreiter for sharing their sailing skills.

Erik Beale, for opening the window on the world of speedsailing.

Gregg and Juliette Blue, for the avocados and warm welcome.

Bernie Brandstaetter and Peter Thommen for patiently showing me the lengthy process of custom fin and board making.

Craig Masonville and Malte Simmer for sharing their first-hand knowledge of high performance windsurfing's history.

Nils Rosenblad, for explaining sail design.

Gaylene Nagel of *Bare Wetsuits*, Kris Bowers of *Oakley*, and Rob Kaplan of *Da Kine Hawaii*, for their kind support.

Thanks also to the talented subjects of my photographs; their dedication and skill made them possible.

Some amongst the many: Mark Angulo, Ian Boyd, Bjorn Dunkerbeck, Dave Kalama, Robby Naish and Jason Polakow.

Introduction

Windsurfing represents an ideal synthesis of man and machine. Few other pastimes can give one a greater sense of freedom or adventure. At every level new challenges are available for those who seek them and yet, even after many years, a cruise is still a pleasure.

I first sailed a sinker in 1983, with some six years of windsurfing experience behind me. Leaving the beach, I was on top of the world, that is until I fell trying to gybe and was unceremoniously washed up on the beach some time later. Books of the day did not go much further than how to rail ride or tack; those seeking the limits were on their own.

Now, there are many avenues to learning. Experienced instructors teach students to waterstart in a matter of hours. Video cassettes, books and magazines are available showing top sailors in action.

Do not be discouraged if your first attempts are frustrating, as everybody has to start somewhere. Approach learning one step at a time; the sailors in this book have spent years honing their abilities. The most important blocks to achievement are usually inner ones: that fear of letting go and just doing it.

Study the photo sequences very carefully. It has been proven that athletes who train by visualizing (imagining or, if you like, imaging) the movements involved, progress almost as fast as those physically doing the moves.

Selecting the best conditions for training will make improvement quicker. Learning to waterstart and gybe will be easier on an enclosed estuary or other protected water than on the open sea. Steady wind also helps.

An important point, often overlooked, is that it is possible to think too much and try too hard. While writing this book I would sometimes try to talk myself through moves as I did them; the results were usually disastrous. Actions that were second nature suddenly became incredibly difficult when my intellect got in the way of the intuitive side of my brain. The answer seems to be: give your mind room to do what it already knows.

1
The Quiver

The first record that I can find of anybody windsurfing dates back to the 1940s, when Tom Blake, a legendary surfing pioneer from Oahu, Hawaii, first attached a sail to his huge wooden surfboard. He would sail off Waikiki beach, and then roll up his sail to surf back in.

Sailsurfing fell into obscurity after those early days. It was reinvented when, in 1967, Hoyle Sweitzer and Jim Drake connected a sail to a surfboard with a universal joint. The rest, as they say, is history.

Initially there were few boards on the market and few choices to be made in equipment; a 'storm' sail of around 4.2sq m (45sq ft) or a high wind daggerboard (smaller and more swept back than the stock daggerboard) to ease handling in strong winds, were about the only options.

As is common in a young sport, windsurfing equipment went

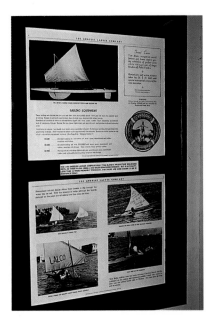

Fig 2   A brochure showing 'production' sailing boards. Only a few were made and none are known to still exist.

through a fast, exciting period of evolution. Developments came about in rapid succession as enthusiastic sailors continually pushed the limits of their new sport.

A group of young sailors who chose Hawaii as their home created major innovations. Many were also surfers, keen to take their sailboards into the waves. Their stock

12ft (3.7m) boards proved unwieldy so they started cutting them down by literally chopping off the back. To help maintain control in the air, Larry Stanley and Mike Horgan attached footstraps to their boards and others soon followed. The other real breakthrough came when Mike Waltz, Malte Simmer and others, started scrounging old surfboards to sail on. The smaller boards proved the best option in the surf.

Rig design was modified to survive the new environment. Stronger aluminium replaced broken laminated teak booms, and sails were heavily reinforced, with shorter booms for the surf. Borrowing ideas from catamaran sails, full-length battens were added, although at first only to the top of the sail. Malte

Fig 3   An original Baja board made by Hoyle Sweitzer. This model preceded the original mass-production board, the 'Windsurfer'.

Fig 1   This board is a hollow surfboard similar to those Tom Blake first attached a sail to at Waikiki. The small photographs on the wall show early rigs.

Simmer, who was then working for the sailmakers Barry Spanier and Geoff Bourne – and sleeping under the cutting table in the loft – was the first to make these work. These adaptations made sailing possible in big surf and high winds.

Today, people windsurf everywhere where there is wind and water, and the market provides a choice of equipment for practically any combination. Being spoilt for choice has its downside, this being that making the right purchase is no simple task. Increasing your knowledge and understanding your specific needs makes buying less of a gamble.

One of the best ways to test equipment is to take a vacation at a resort set up especially for windsurfing. Many centres also have qualified instructors able to provide sound advice on equipment. For those whose windsurfing time is limited to a few weeks a year, this may be the best alternative. Just as ski resorts have shops full of top ski gear, more and more windsurfing locations offer the same service.

The following is a brief rundown on high-performance equipment.

BOARDS

Course Boards

The largest boards are course boards. These are race boards for light to medium winds. Most are about 12ft 6in (3.8m) long with adjustable mast tracks and a centreboard. Since they are easily uphauled in light wind, many people purchase a course board as their first board.

Course boards are raced in 10–14kn of wind. (A knot is 1 nautical mile per hour.) In stronger breezes, racers switch to much smaller boards, around 9ft (2.75m), known as course-slaloms. The latest sails are so efficient that racers plane all the way around the course, making the extra volume of a larger board redundant.

Slalom Boards

In slalom competition, racers reach back and forth between marks without having to sail upwind. This is what slalom boards do best. Slalom boards are perhaps the fastest growing part of the windsurfing market.

The boards used in slalom have no centreboard. They are very fast and quite easy to turn. Many sailors buy slalom boards as their first high-performance board. A slalom board is the right choice for sailors who love speed. They are very exciting in strong winds, although not recommended for waves.

Be careful when buying your first slalom board, as some are hard to sail. Be sure to try before you buy. Remember that problems may be

Fig 4   A modern course-slalom board, shaped by Peter Thommen. Its bottom is quite flat with a slight amount of vee noticeable in the tail. The hard chine improves windward performance.

Fig 5   Slalom racing in the surf at Ho'okipa Maui.

the result of using the incorrect fin and not the board's fault.

The latest slalom boards have very simple bottom shapes – flat in the nose, going to a slight vee in the tail. Earlier designs for slalom and speed boards had concaves or channels (concaves look like ripples on the bottom of the board) to make a board come on to a plane quickly. With better sails, racers plane all the way around the course, making top end speed the primary requirement.

There is a big variation in the size of boards designed for slalom; wind and sea conditions and the size of the sailor must be considered. Common lengths for slalom boards range between 8ft 6in–9ft 2in (2.6–2.8m).

Wave Boards

In surf, a wave board is essential, as slalom equipment is simply too hard to manoeuvre for wave riding. Wave boards can be a good choice for all-round short board sailing.

They are easy to waterstart and steer, and ideal for learning advanced moves such as jump gybes and duck tacks.

Fig 6   Racers keep many sails rigged in case of changes in wind or sea conditions.

Boards need to be low volume for riding waves. Big boards are almost impossible to surf on (unless you are as skilled as Robby Naish who has been known to loop a course board). The reason for this is that your speed increases dramatically on the wave and, while a large board may be easy to sail out, it will prove uncontrollable on the wave face.

Wave boards range in size between around 7ft 8in–8ft 10in (2.3–2.7m).

A Closer Look at Design

Understanding design fundamentals makes buying a board easier.

Basic knowledge can provide a defence against sales hype and costly mistakes.

THE PLAN FORM

The plan form is the shape or outline of a board as viewed from above. For boards of the same length, the shape of the tail is a big factor in determining the ease with which a board will gybe and how fast it will go. Narrow tails are better for high speeds and long drawn-out turns. Speed boards are particularly narrow to reduce drag and improve control in a straight line.

Fig 7 This board has a rounded pin tail – the most versatile shape for wave riding.

Fig 8 Robby Naish in the surf at Ho'okipa, Maui.

For wave sailing, the optimum shape depends on the waves and the wind on the day, and the rider's technique. For general use, rounded pin tails are the most popular.

ASYMMETRICAL BOARDS

Asymmetrical boards, as the name implies, are shaped differently on each side. The cutback side is shorter, with a square tail for rapid off-the-lip turns; the other side is longer and narrow for control in high-speed bottom turns. Asymmetrical designs are popular for locations with big surf and trade winds that blow consistently from the same direction.

Fig 9 An asymmetrical board, attached to the feet of Ian Boyd.

To find out more about the origins of asymmetrical boards back in 1983, I spoke to Malte Simmer and Craig Masonville who are two of the best and most photographed sailors in the 1980s. This is what Malte said:

Back then, everybody – Mike Waltz, Robby Naish and all the other guys – were surfing with their back foot out of the strap and I wanted to keep mine in. Craig Masonville came up with a shape resembling a can-opener, which was the first asymmetrical board to really work. With the asymmetrical shape, your heel is closer to the back corner of the board when surfing, and you can keep your foot in the strap.

The following is what Craig told me:

Asymmetric boards have been around forever in surfing. Malte and Matt Schweitzer, I think, tried boards which were symmetric in shape except for a cutout in the tail. I decided to make a board which was completely asymmetric – rails, rocker vee, everything. When I shaped the first one I was really broke and I thought that I'd wasted my money on a $60 blank. I got depressed looking at it and then I glassed it and got even more depressed. When I went down to the beach everybody laughed but then I took it on the water and it just worked great. The first one had a 9in [30cm] and then the next a 12in (30.5cm) cutout. The latest models have cutouts ranging from about 6–12in [15–30.5cm]. In perfect sideshore winds, the longer the cutout is, the better. It is more noticeable on wider boards, though you can still feel the difference on a gunny board.

VEE

Harder to see than the general outline of a board is the degree of vee in the bottom. Looking at the bottom of the board, the centreline will be slightly higher than the edges. This difference is described as vee.

The manner in which water flows along the bottom of a board affects both speed and control. The flat to vee shape that is common on slalom and speed boards provides a better working environment for the fin. Water flows away from it, thus improving the efficiency of the foil and making boards easier to control. With the powerful sails available today, this is an important factor.

Vee also makes a board 'looser', i.e. easier to turn. For this reason, wave boards have more vee than slalom boards.

ROCKER

The upturned nose of a board (its nose rocker) prevents it from digging in or purling when riding over waves or choppy water. Harder to see is the slight upturn of the tail on most boards. The tail rocker makes boards easier to turn. Wave boards have more rocker than race boards, and for this reason they also ride more smoothly.

Rocker also provides another function: when planing, a racer rocks back on the tail, reducing the planing surface and drag. The optimum rocker profile makes a board very fast.

While the rocker of different boards can be compared by placing them side by side, a board can best be judged by how it rides through the water, not how it looks on the floor. Some designers photograph and videotape their prototypes from moving boats to study performances objectively.

VOLUME

A thicker board is more buoyant. A board too thick for your weight will bounce over chop and be uncomfortable to sail. The rails will fail to dig in while turning, making gybing difficult as well. Since most boards are sold to people who sail on lakes, the majority of production boards are large. If you are getting into wave sailing, I recommend investigating custom boards available from local shapers.

RAILS

The edges of your board are called the rails. Rail shape affects the ease with which a board will go upwind and turn. They can be described as hard or soft. A soft rail is rounded. The roundness helps your board grip the water and makes the rail less likely to catch while turning. Wave boards have soft, thin rails for much of their length.

Hard rails create less drag and provide lateral resistance, which is helpful when going to windward. Slalom and race boards have hard boxy rails. To make race boards easier to handle, the edge is usually slightly rounded. This is described as tuck or bevel and can be difficult to see for the untrained eye. A bevelled rail can still be fast while aiding control in turns.

Funboards

No discussion of boards would be complete without mentioning funboards. The term was created as a marketing gambit in Germany and can mean practically any board with footstraps. Entry level funboards are those of about 10ft 6in (3.15m). They are basically big slalom boards with retractable centreboards and adjustable mast tracks.

These are a good choice as an all-round board for a lighter sailor in winds of force 3 and above. For reaching in strong winds, keep the centreboard all the way up and the mast track all the way back. To go upwind in lighter breezes, drop the centreboard and move the mast forward.

They are a popular choice as a first board for learning advanced manoeuvres such as carve gybes, but too large for wave sailing.

The Right Board

There is no such thing as the perfect board for all people in all conditions. In general, larger sailors and

Fig 10 In preparation for a wave contest, Robby Naish has four boards on the beach ready to go. Variations in waves and wind strength will determine which he will use.

lighter winds require more voluminous boards. In strong winds, body weight is less of a factor, and small boards are best for everybody, even heavyweights. The most important thing is to have a board that you can control.

CUSTOM BOARD CONSTRUCTION

Most serious racers and wave sailors use custom equipment to match their style, size and the conditions perfectly. To learn more about construction I visited Peter Thommen, the principal shaper for F2 and World Cup champions, Bjorn and Britt Dunkerbeck among others. Peter works in a small workshop in Hawaii producing state of the art equipment. He shares his office with Bernie Brandstaetter, an ex-

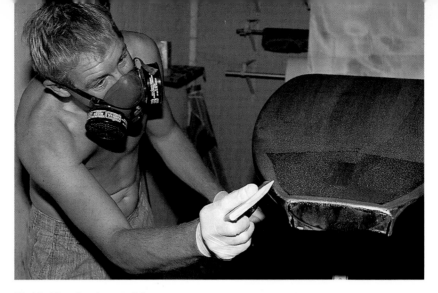

Fig 12 The glass is wetted down thoroughly. Carbon fibre is added to the fin box area for strength, as this board is very light. (Demonstrated by Adrian Roper.)

World Cup racer from Austria who designs and shapes fins.

Peter Thommen says this:

The main thing we are looking at in board design now is trying to reduce drag. You need your board to get up to speed and you have to manoeuvre. Once you are at speed you do not need a board – you can barefoot waterski, so you don't need any surface. You try to make a board whose surface can be reduced to a bare minimum.

These days you have to develop everything together, otherwise it might not work. It is pretty obvious that Bjorn's sails are working pretty fine with my boards. When I give my boards to somebody who is using a different sail, they have problems in some conditions. The boards tend to stick to the water, hitting the chop all the time, and going upwind especially. Bjorn doesn't have that problem. It depends on the pocket of the sail – some sails create more lift than others. When you have a sail that creates just forward push but also some lift you can probably go with a straighter rocker line. Some sails let the draft wander backwards so you can load the fin more, and you have sails where the draft stays

really locked into the front and you can't load the fin that much.

Peter's boards are deceptively simple to look at – the bottom is basically flat, to a slight vee in the tail. They are of a composite construction. The core is a piece of 0.5kg (1lb) density styrofoam, which is laminated to a thin bottom layer of 2.3kg (5lb) density divina cell foam. A layer of fibreglass between the two pieces of foam adds structural support.

Once the blank (the core of the finished board) is shaped, it is wrapped with layers of carbon-fibre cloth. The fin box, mast box and footstrap inserts are installed. Finally the board is finish-sanded and painted. Epoxy resin is used throughout.

SAILS

As with boards, there is a considerable selection of sails available. Where and how you sail will determine what is best for you. For maximum speed, race sails with camber inducers (small joints that connect the battens to the masts) and wide luff sleeves are necessary. For easy handling, wave sails are best. If you want something that offers control and speed on your shortboard, take a look at a wave slalom, especially one with battens or camber in-

Fig 11 A power planer takes off the bulk of the excess material. This is a noisy task, so hearing protection is essential. (Demonstrated by Peter Thommen.)

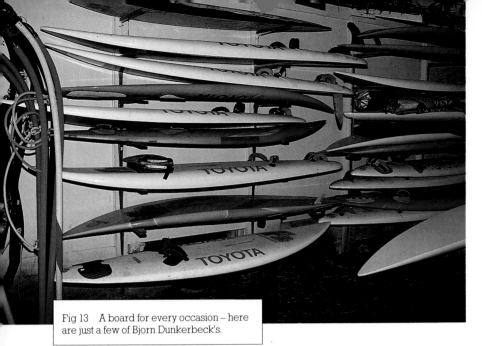

Fig 13 A board for every occasion – here are just a few of Bjorn Dunkerbeck's.

ducers that can be changed to alter the sail's characteristics.

When selecting a new sail, it is important for it to be compatible with the rest of your equipment. The flex of your mast must match the curve of the sail's luff. Race sails require stiff aluminium or carbon masts for efficiency. Putting too stiff a mast on a small wave sail makes it unstable and powerless during lulls in the wind. Check with your dealer or the sail manufacturer.

Sails are made from a variety of materials, mostly polyester- and mylar-based, with windows usually made of PVC. Every year, designers try to find materials that are lighter and stronger. Lighter materials are especially important above the booms, owing to the leverage factor. One material used in race and some high-performance wave sails is called 'Monofilm'. This clear material is very resistant to stretching and much lighter than conventional mylar/Dacron sailcloth. Unfortunately, Monofilm is less durable, although small tears can be easily repaired with tape.

Fig 14 Deanna Kearz is shown here hand-cutting a custom sail.

In future years, sails may be popped out of a mould like so many jellybeans; at the moment they are usually cut by computer-operated machines and sewn by skilled machine operators.

Most sails have adjustments at the mast-head to enable them to be used on different-sized masts. Using a long mast on a sail with a short luff is not recommended. For easy handling, most sails require the mast tip to flex when hit by a gust. A long extension places the top of the sail in a stiffer part of the mast. One solution is to use a shorter mast, placing the top of the

sail at the mast head. When cutting a mast down in size, make sure that the booms will still be attached in the area of mast reinforcement.

Wave Sails

Surf requires sails that are easy to handle. The best wave sails are both powerful enough for jumping and flat enough for speeding down the face of a wave. Wave sails must be easy to depower when necessary and need to be well reinforced.

Most wave sails are 'RAFs'. The term RAF means rotating asymmetrical foil. Designed with closely fitting mast sleeves, the battens rotate about the mast to provide better foil entry.

Some manufacturers make sails with convertible battens. You can remove camber inducers or change full-length battens for leach battens. Changing a sail's batten configurations will alter its performance, making the same sail either easier to handle or more powerful.

Race Sails

Race sails are particularly difficult

Fig 15 Broken equipment is not uncommon in the surf; masts are particularly vulnerable.

Fig 16 This prototype race sail is being tested by Simmer Style sail designer Nils Rosenblad.

to design. They require easy handling, good acceleration and a high top speed. Camber inducers help to create a powerful leading edge.

Since racers rarely come off-plane, race sails are designed, like the boards, for top speed more than acceleration. The main body of the sails is deep and powerful and the head is flat and designed to twist off in gusts.

Speed Sails

Fewer restrictions apply to speed sails, which are designed exclusively for performance off the wind on flat water. Speed sails have many battens to make their foil shape very stable in high winds.

FINS

The quickest way to change how a board handles is to change fins. On the shelf most fins look like they will do the job. You could use just about any fin if you had to. For top performance, however, the right fin is essential. The first thing that you might notice (after seeing that they come in every colour under the sun) is that fins take on many different shapes and sizes. Fins, like boards, can be easily classified according to their use. Different fins are made for speed, slalom, wave and course sailing.

Requirements for a fin moving at 12kn differ from those at 25kn. When looking at a fin, consider its plan form and foil shape. Plan form

refers to the side view, a fin's width and height. Foil shape would be easiest seen if the fin was sliced through horizontally.

Plan form creates lateral resistance, and the foil shape lift. Upright fins – the most efficient shape for pointing – are slower at turning than swept-back fins. They are used on course and slalom boards. According to Bernie Brandstaetter (an F2 designer who makes fins for Bjorn Dunkerbeck and many other racers) narrow elliptical foils seem

Fig 18 A display of fins – the first few are slot fins.

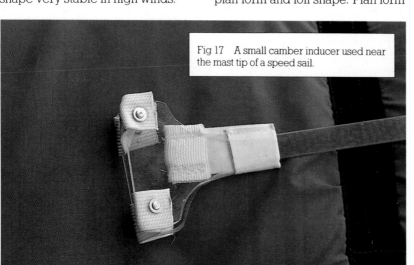

Fig 17 A small camber inducer used near the mast tip of a speed sail.

to work best on race boards. They are very efficient and relatively easy to control.

Course boards use the same fins as slalom boards, but in a larger size. When changing to a smaller board and sail in increasing wind, you need a smaller fin as well. All the parts must work together.

Wave sailing – with its high-speed transitions and radical moves – requires fins that are easy to control. Almost all wave fins are dolphin-shaped. Dolphin-shaped fins twist off more easily and are the easiest shape to gybe. Wave fins must still not slow you down too much, but be able to take you back upwind.

A few years ago, wave fins with small fore-fins known as 'canards' were common. Now fins with slots in the leading edge have been found to work better and are popular with many sailors. Both developments came about to reduce spinout. Spinout results from the loss of attached flow from the leeward side of the fin, causing the tail of your board to move rapidly sideways. Slots increase the maximum angle of attack, making it easier to re-establish flow. A sensitive sailor will generally feel a spinout about to happen and can recover, but if spinout is a continual problem for you, try changing fins.

Some wave boards work best with additional tiny fins near the rail called thrusters.

The construction material is a primary consideration for fin designers. If the end product is either stiffer or more flexible than the prototype it will not behave the same. When loaded, a fin twists at the tip. The stiffness of the fin and its shape affects this twist. This is another reason why a swept-back wave fin is more manoeuvrable than a slalom fin.

Fig 19   The small fins near the rails of this high-flying board are thrusters.

Finally, fin choice is a personal matter. Try different fins to see which work best for you.

Fin Positioning

If your board has a regular fin box, you can adjust the location by a few inches. Even a small change affects performance.

Fins placed in a forward position make a board looser or easier to turn. A more aft location stiffens up handling and makes the board track better, improving directional stability.

The original fin box came to windsurfers from surfboards. Its design is adequate for the sideways' stresses put on at low speeds or for wave sailing but not for high-speed slalom or course boards. Standard fin boxes are shallow and put all the load on to a strip of fibreglass or plastic less than 1in (2.5cm) deep.

Foil designer, Larry Tuttle, came up with a design, known as the 'Tuttle box', that puts the fin base all the way through the board. This is a stiffer and stronger arrangement. The only drawback to this particular system is that the fin cannot be moved.

FOOTSTRAPS

On shortboards, these are a necessity to maintain control at high speeds. They should fit tightly over the ball of your foot. Loose footstraps, which allow the foot to slide in too far, increase the risk of injury.

With feet firmly attached to the board, you will have greater control and be more sensitive to its motion over the water. Practice increases this sensitivity and in time your board begins to feel more like an extension of your legs than like a separate entity.

On a slalom or wave board three straps are enough, although you may choose to have a double strap at the rear. Course boards require many more straps. Since there are so many, a lot of racers use special lightweight straps for most of them.

The Location of Footstraps

The location of footstraps on your board makes a big difference in board performance, affecting both maximum speed and control.

If the footstraps are too far forward, a board will be easy to control, but gybes will tend to be

19

Fig 20(a)   This strap is too loose.

Fig 20(b)   When correctly adjusted, the strap should hold your foot firmly over the ball.

HARNESSES

Sailing a shortboard is strenuous. In strong winds, few people can stay on the water for long without harnesses. Dingy sailors have had harnesses for a long time, but it took a while before the first windsurfers began to use them. Harnesses were not even permitted on the first Olympic sailboard, the Windglider. Now almost everybody sails with one. They can be worn on the chest, waist or seat. The correct harness depends on the type of sailing that you do. Thickly padded chest harnesses will take some of the sting out of landing on your back when learning loops. Seat harnesses are best used with race sails.

WETSUITS

Modern wetsuit design allows sailors to be comfortable all year round. The appropriate suit is a worthwhile investment and should last many years. For extreme conditions, drysuits, or semi-drysuits, are necessary. Windsurfing versions are close-fitting yet allow room for arm expansion and mobility. Neoprene hats and booties will keep extremities toasty.

Fig 21   Waist and chest harnesses are preferred amongst wave sailors for their manageability and ease of hooking in and out. This harness, worn by Kelby Anno, is typical.

In moderate climates, steamers – a one-piece design adapted from surfing – are great. Those made for windsurfing have expandable or removable sleeves. The warmest steamers have glued seams to prevent water seepage. Vests or spring suits, with short sleeves and legs, are suitable in warmer climes.

To be efficient, a suit must fit

long and drawn out; too far back and a board will not point well. In high winds the nose will feel very light and tend to bounce out of the water when broad reaching. Performance in lower wind speeds will be affected also.

Though your straps may feel perfectly placed on your present board, those same locations may not work on a different board. It is not unusual for a pro sailor to move the straps once or twice on a new board to find the ideal position. The slight weight increase of extra inserts is worth it.

Fig 22   Race boards require a different stance, making seat harnesses the choice. Bjorn Dunkerbeck here in perfect form.

Fig 23   A well-fitting neoprene vest for warmer weather.

well. When purchasing, pay attention to detail. Look for the following features:

- A close-fitting single-lined neoprene collar
- Leg and arm seals
- Glued and blind-stitched seams on cold-water suits
- Strong zippers
- Extra layers on hard-wearing areas, such as the seat and knees

SUN-GLASSES

Many racers wear sun-glasses while on the racecourse as well as on the beach. Lake/beach environments require special-purpose lenses. In particular they should block out all UVB (the most dangerous wavelength) and most UVA. To prevent eye-strain, be sure to buy glasses that are optically correct.

HELMETS

Using a helmet is a good idea when sailing in crowded waters, in very strong winds or when learning loops. If you buy a helmet, choose a hard-shell model that is lightweight and floats. Of course, make sure that it fits well too.

WORLD CUP EQUIPMENT

World Cup sailors need to travel with an incredible amount of gear to be competitive in all conditions. Competing in all three disciplines can mean travelling with a minimum of seven and a maximum of twelve boards.

Since course boards are only used in a limited wind range, one is enough. There is a rule forbidding racing in less than 11kn and when the wind gets stronger than a steady 13–14kn, sailors switch to course-slalom boards.

For a large variety of conditions, four slalom and course-slalom boards are needed, and for waves another four boards may get to travel. A quiver of race and wave sails, assorted fins and masts, also make the trip. Check-in desk staff are as delighted as the porters – they have been known to hide at the sight of a World Cup sailor.

These days, most sailors are independent and must take care of themselves. The days of large, fully supported factory teams are over. The equipment itself is custom-made for the racers. Most companies use the World Cup sailors to test and develop their product. Similar sails may be available to the public the next year, but it can take two years or more for a new board design to be put on the shelves.

MAINTENANCE

Windsurfing equipment is made from very durable plastics and synthetics, and with a little common sense, it is easy to care for. These materials are sensitive to ultraviolet light, so keep your gear out of the sun when not using it. After sailing in salt water, rinse everything in fresh water and leave it to dry in the shade before storing for any long periods of time. If stored wet, the material used in sail windows is more likely to fog. When packing up your sail, roll it up instead of folding to avoid creasing the mylar or monofilm.

The old saying, 'A stitch in time saves nine', applies to windsurf equipment as well. Any dings in your board should be repaired immediately to prevent water absorption, saving costly repairs later, due to delamination. Ultra-light polystyrene boards are especially susceptible. When holed, they soak up water like sponges. Be sure to let water drain out and give the foam time to dry before patching. Sails with small holes can often be repaired with strong plastic tape or stickers. Larger holes, blown-out mast sleeves, batten pockets and the like, require professional repair.

Scraped fins should be patched with fibreglass resin and wet-sanded with 400 grit paper. Handy repair kits are available for fins with broken tabs (if you still have the fin). Keep an eye out for frayed lines because replacing them when necessary can save you a long swim some day.

The sport of windsurfing has grown and diversified. It will be interesting to see what the next twenty years will bring. Improved materials are sure to come up, making everything lighter and more efficient. Whatever equipment you have available, the most important thing is to get out there and use it. Enjoy yourself and don't get too hung up on the latest gimmick.

2
Basics

Attempts to improve your windsurfing will be more successful if you practise under the right conditions – initially, steady wind and smooth water. As your skill and confidence improve, you will try more challenging conditions. At first, standing up and gybing without falling will be challenge enough.

At this stage, professional instruction is recommended. Group lessons can be great, as just seeing problems from a different perspective can be most enlightening.

Further along in this book there are many difficult manoeuvres, some of which even the top pros rarely complete. If you wish to progress to that level or even if you just want to have fun on a Sunday afternoon, you will learn faster if you approach each new move one step at a time. If you are having problems, go back to what you can already do and build on that. You will progress faster and be less frustrated. Our muscles also have memories and bad habits can be very difficult to unlearn; be patient and consistent.

A final point to consider: while this book is full of helpful advice I don't recommend trying to think too hard while on the water. Pay very close attention to the photo sequences and try to imagine yourself as the sailor, perhaps even feeling your muscles flex as you recreate the moves in your mind. Many top athletes do this instinctively; others may learn it from sports psychologists. Either way, as I've said before, the technique has been proven to work.

CURRENTS AND TIDES

Many people start windsurfing in protected waters with little or no current. Shortboard sailing is made for high winds and waves. If you are starting to sail a shortboard and are unfamiliar with these conditions, there are a few things that should be known.

The current in tidal waters is usually predictable and changes direction with the tide, which turns every twelve hours. Most places in the world have tide charts which are easily available, either in the local press, from the harbour master, or the weather office.

Conditions in tidal waters can vary dramatically from hour to hour. Waves will change with the tide, as their size is affected by the depth of the water and the current. Reefs can become too shallow to sail over and hidden pilings near old piers may emerge. A break with great sailing at low tide may be non-existent at high. Check the tide tables or ask around before heading out in the surf. Also, spend some time observing local conditions and ask sailors familiar with the spot, what, if any, are the hazards.

Not only tidal waters have waves. Many large rivers can offer excellent shortboard sailing conditions. Having the current against the wind is the best situation for windsurfing. This makes it easy to stay upwind and makes strong wind feel even stronger. With the wind against the current, even a river can provide large waves; the well known Columbia River Gorge in the United States is a perfect example of this.

Rip Tides

Water deposited on the beach must drain back into the sea. Since the contours of the beach act as valleys and hills, directing the flow, the outgoing water is compressed into a smaller space and flows faster than the water coming in. This strong outflow of water is known as a rip. A current of 6–10kn is common at many popular wave spots. Knowing where the current is strongest can save a lot of grief.

It is essential to be aware of rip tides or other strong currents before heading out, because they can be impossible to swim against. If you do need to swim in and find yourself making no headway, don't panic and waste energy fighting the rip, swim parallel with the beach to get out of the outflowing current and try again further along. The current can prove advantageous, too, as it is sometimes helpful in keeping you and your equipment off the rocks.

APPARENT WIND

The force you feel on your sail is called the apparent wind. The apparent wind is affected by your motion through the water and the current. Here is an example: If you are sailing in a 5kn current that is going in the opposite direction of a 20kn wind, the force that your sail feels will be the equivalent of a 25kn breeze in calm water. If the wind and current are in the same direction, it will feel like you are sailing in a breeze of only 15kn.

Apparent wind not only moves at a different velocity from the true wind but also comes from a different direction. This is especially true at high speeds, when the wind feels to your sail as if you are close-hauled, even though the true wind is coming from astern.

Another example of apparent wind can be felt when sailing down the face of a wave. Going out you may be just making it through and yet once on the wave you are overpowered. This is common when sailing big surf in light winds, and makes the choice of sail more difficult. For this reason, wave sails are less powerful and more forgiving than race sails.

Apparent wind can be used to your advantage. If you have good speed going into a gybe, there will be little apparent wind in your sail when pointing downwind, making flipping the rig easier.

RIGGING

Using the correct sail and board makes learning easier. Your rig also needs to be set up for your size and for the conditions of the day. To help decide, check out what sail size other people are using, taking their weight into consideration. Short-boards are very sensitive to having the correct power-to-weight ratio and 1sq m (10.76sq ft) in size makes a big difference. Once rigged, you can change the power in your sail with the outhaul and downhaul, but you cannot make a 6sq m (64.6sq ft) sail feel like a 4.5sq m (48.4sq ft).

Be careful if the wind is offshore. It may seem calm at the beach but be blowing far stronger 100m (110yd) out. Onshore winds can look and feel stronger than they really are. This is where experience at a particular location will pay off. The rig is the motor that drives your board. A well-rigged sail is more efficient and easier to sail.

In Fig 24, Christine Spreiter demonstrates how to rig your board.

Fig 24(a) Unroll your sail.

Fig 24(b) The more flexible end of a batten is rigged closest to the mast.

Fig 24(c) There are two standard mast sizes. Some mast/base combinations require an extra sleeve which acts as a shim. Plastic bottles or tubing can be used as a replacement if necessary. It is important that there be no slack between the mast and its base. Some masts also require a reinforcing shim at the booms.

Fig 24(d) Slip the mast into its sleeve.

Fig 24(e)   Smaller sails have adjustable heads. Completely rig the sail to determine the correct adjustment.

Fig 24(f)   Downhaul your sail enough to pull out all horizontal wrinkles and then downhaul about 3cm (1in) more.

Fig 24(g)   The right setting at the mast head places the tack (the bottom corner of the sail) very close to the cleat when fully downhauled.

Fig 24(h)   Most booms are clamped to the mast with buckles.

Fig 24(i)   Make sure the outhaul runs unobstructed.

Fig 24(j)   Legs again save the day. Outhauls have less tension on them than downhauls.

Fig 24(k)   The boom end should be adjusted close to the clew.

Fig 24(l)   Attach the rig to the board.

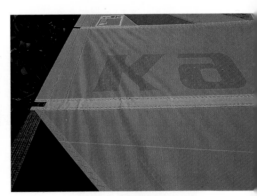

Fig 24(m)   Battens pockets should be wrinkle free.

Fig 24(n)   Stand your sail up and try it out.

Fig 24(q)   Try the sail on both tacks.

Fig 24(o)   Adjust the boom height if necessary.

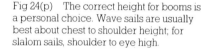

Fig 24(p)   The correct height for booms is a personal choice. Wave sails are usually best about chest to shoulder height; for slalom sails, shoulder to eye high.

Boom Height

The first rigging task is to establish the correct boom height. The easiest way to do this is to attach your mast to its base, and hold it upright on your board. Stand beside your mast and note where you will be attaching your booms.

For a wave board, the standard height is approximately chest level. On a slalom board, eye or forehead level is appropriate. Once you have sailed your board and found the settings that are most comfortable, marking them with a waterproof pen for future reference is a smart idea. Some racers (who switch equipment often) even use a measuring tape to check the height of their booms.

The correct boom height is also determined by performance. In light winds, rigging booms a little higher makes sails feel more powerful. In stronger wind, rigging lower lets the sail twist off when hit by a gust and also puts more weight on your harness for extra power.

BASIC TUNING

Do not worry about the occasional crease, but make sure that you have downhauled enough. Insufficient downhaul tension is a common error. Lack of tension makes sails unstable, causing the draft and centre of effort to move aft when hit by a gust.

If your sail seems large enough but lacks power, or the power switches on and off unevenly, try letting off the outhaul a touch. Should the feeling persist, try the sail on a softer mast. Never set a sail totally flat nor so full that it touches the leeward boom.

Always adjust outhaul and downhaul in unison to keep the sail balanced.

Note When testing your sail in light wind, wrinkles in the window are normal and not a sign of an ill-tuned sail.

Methods

Fig 26   Shortboards are light and easy to carry.

Fig 27   Robby Naish shows the standard method: the board is held with the windward footstrap, the rig with the other hand on the boom.

Fig 28   Supporting the rig on your head is a good way to walk longer distances. Beware of stretching the window material.

Fig 25   Roll up the sail and store it in its bag. Take out any battens that get in the way while rolling, making sure not to lose them!

DE-RIGGING

Small gestures like letting off the downhaul before the outhaul and rinsing your equipment in fresh water, will make your investment last longer.

CARRYING YOUR BOARD

For an assembled shortboard and rig, using any one of three standard methods is recommended.

Fig 29   Carrying everything on the head is another way to walk long distances. It can be tricky getting it all up there but, once in balance, it works well.

Fig 30   Jason Polakow demonstrates the casual Australian approach.

Fig 31(b)   Step into the gap, facing the water. Reach down, taking hold of the windward front footstrap with windward hand. Hold on to the boom near the balance point with your other hand.

Fig 31(a)   Line up the board so that it is across the wind, facing towards the water. Place the rig on the ground with the tip of the mast pointing away from the water and the clew downwind. Leave a gap between the mast and the board.

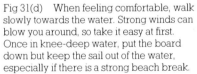

Fig 31(c)   Stand up, taking a second to balance board and rig. If you feel unbalanced, try moving your hands on the booms. Use the wind to help support the weight.

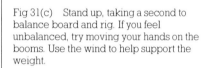

Fig 31(e)   Hold the mast and step around behind your board to prepare to beach- or waterstart. In surf, it is important to keep the sail out of the water when beachstarting.

Fig 31(d)   When feeling comfortable, walk slowly towards the water. Strong winds can blow you around, so take it easy at first. Once in knee-deep water, put the board down but keep the sail out of the water, especially if there is a strong beach break.

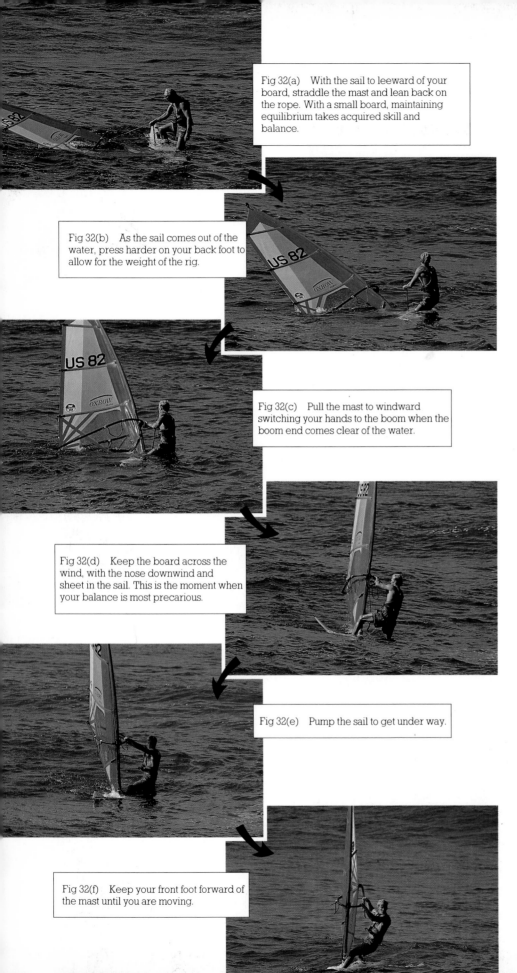

Fig 32(a)   With the sail to leeward of your board, straddle the mast and lean back on the rope. With a small board, maintaining equilibrium takes acquired skill and balance.

Fig 32(b)   As the sail comes out of the water, press harder on your back foot to allow for the weight of the rig.

Fig 32(c)   Pull the mast to windward switching your hands to the boom when the boom end comes clear of the water.

Fig 32(d)   Keep the board across the wind, with the nose downwind and sheet in the sail. This is the moment when your balance is most precarious.

Fig 32(e)   Pump the sail to get under way.

Fig 32(f)   Keep your front foot forward of the mast until you are moving.

UPHAULING

Starting a longboard with the 'rope' is the first thing everybody learns. Because shortboards are so tippy when not moving, good balance is required. If at first you practise on a large board, uphauling smaller boards is not too difficult.

Should the wind become too light to waterstart, uphauling is the only way to sail back to the beach. Uphauling (also called rope start- ing) is an essential skill in big surf too. Behind large waves there is often little wind and the impact zone is no place to be floundering.

WATERSTARTING

Waterstarting is the most important basic move, and enables you to begin using high-performance equipment. You will find that short- boards do not float very well. Learning can be very frustrating at first. To make this manoeuvre easier on yourself, be patient – learn it one step at a time.

Don't expect to jump up on your board and sail immediately. Take frequent breaks and have a think about what you are trying to do – continually repeating the same mistakes is a slow way to learn.

Only try waterstarting when winds are strong, as learning in light winds or with too small a sail will make progress impossible. If you have the choice, choose a location with a sandy bottom and no obstructions or obstacles. Avoid being near swimmers. Initially you will need all the room that you can get. A cross-shore wind is ideal.

Fig 33 (*Opposite*)   Waterstarting is an essential basic skill

Waterstarting involves the following five stages:

1. Positioning your board and rig.
2. Clearing the rig from the water, i.e. flying the rig.
3. Steering your rig and learning to maintain your position.
4. Allowing the sail to drag you through the water with your feet on the board. This is known as body drag.
5. Standing up and sailing away.

Practise on land first. Getting out of the water successfully is so much easier once you have developed a feel for the forces acting on your sail. On the beach, with the fin in the sand, line up everything as if in the water. Sit on the sand, with your sail overhead, and imagine you are sailing. Try pumping the sail, moving it in and out in a rowing action. Pumping gives a feeling for when the rig is in balance and will lift you out of the water.

Positioning the Rig

Before trying to get up, your board should be perpendicular (90 degrees) to the wind. To be able to get the sail out of the water, everything needs to be in the right place. Predictably, your sail will be pointing the wrong way when you fall in. Repositioning it may involve flipping the sail over or swimming.

Just like a kite, your sail will continue to fly if you keep it at the right angle to the wind. You need to

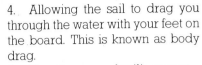

Fig 34(a)   Imagine yourself sailing while sitting in the sand with your rig overhead. Grasping the basics on land will save considerable time on the water.

Fig 34(b)   Place both feet on the board. Feel the energy of the wind in the sail.

Fig 34(c)   When you feel a gust of wind lifting you, sheet in and stand up.

Fig 34(d)   Stay on the board for a while, still imagining yourself sailing.

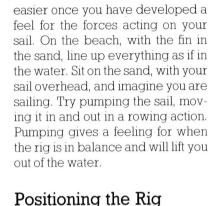

Figs 35(a) and (b)   Flip your sail over if the clew is facing into the wind. By lifting up on the end of the boom, while treading water, the wind will catch under the sail and flip it for you.

Flying the Rig

Fig 37(a)   To fly the rig, hold your mast with one hand just above the booms.

Fig 36   Your board should be perpendicular (90 degrees) to the wind. Align the mast parallel with the board, the tip of your mast pointing in the same direction as the back of your board and the clew of your sail pointing away from the wind. This may require swimming.

maintain the board pointing across the wind and the sail over your head.

Steering

Once you have the hang of flying your rig, practise turning the board using the sail. Similarly to steering a longboard, pushing the mast forwards – towards the front or nose of the board – will move the nose downwind; leaning the mast back towards the tail of the board will move the nose upwind. Before trying the next step, learn to keep the board perpendicular to the wind.

Hold the booms, first with your front hand still on the mast and your back hand 60cm (15in) back. Now place your front hand 15–20cm (5–8in) back of the mast.

You will need to sheet in enough to keep your head above water. Sheet in with your back hand and push up with your front hand (the one closest to your mast). If you feel like you are fighting your rig, it could be that you are trying to push up with both hands, and not just the front one.

Fig 37(b)   Pull the rig over the back of the board, while sinking the tail with your other hand. Having a floatier board makes this step easier as you are using the flotation of the board to lift the sail. Let the water drain off your sail. If the back of your boom has sunk, swim everything towards the wind.

Fig. 37(c)   For the next part, it helps if you can picture your sail as a big kite. Your intention is to make it fly. Simultaneously pull your mast towards you and lift it up overhead. This may require some force.

Body Drag

If until now you have been in shallow water where you can touch the bottom (not an unwise move), you should lift your feet and tread water with them in front of you. Support yourself by sheeting in as you place your back foot up on to the board. Your heel should be just forward of your rear footstrap and on the centreline or slightly to windward. Then put your front foot on to the board and let yourself be dragged along. Rest your feet on it gently, as if you push against it you will turn into the wind, which will drop the sail on to your head.

This is a good time to feel the power in the sail. Experience will teach you to feel when the sail is trimmed correctly. Pulling too much with your back hand stalls the air flow; too little and the sail luffs. Luffing while waterstarting turns the nose of your board into the wind, which flattens you again.

Fig 38   When everything is in balance, let yourself be pulled along by the wind.

Standing Up

If you are the impatient type, you have probably already tried to sail away a few times. Once the first four steps have been mastered, this should not prove too difficult.

As you sail away, you will need to control your rig as you did in the water. Look for the sweet spot in the sail where you will get pulled along in the right direction.

Fig 39(a)   With one foot on the board (some people are more comfortable starting with their front foot on first, others the back, so try both), tread water with your other foot.

Fig 39(b)   Bend your knee to bring the tail of the board underneath you, sinking the tail as you bring it closer. Keep the board from turning into the wind by maintaining your front arm extended forward to windward.

Fig 39(c)   Pump the sail once or twice to make sure that your rig is in balance and then sheet in to get lifted up out of the water.

34

Fig 40   Bjorn Dunkerbeck waterstarting in light wind. Holding the mast with one hand and the boom with the other makes getting out of the water easier.

Waterstarting on the Opposite Tack

Before happily sailing away, practise waterstarting on the tack needed to get back to the beach. All manoeuvres feel different on each tack.

Fig 39(d)   Now step up on to your board as if you were climbing a stair.

Fig 39(e)   Congratulations! You have just waterstarted.

SELF-RESCUE

Should you happen to break down or run out of wind on a large board, it is usually possible to roll up the sail and paddle in. The realities of shortboard sailing are somewhat different. For one thing, the equipment is very strong and usually only breaks under extreme stress. The chances are you will be in waves if you do break something. If running out of wind is the problem, you might possibly be able to roll up your sail but it is difficult to balance all your gear and yourself on a small board while paddling in through the surf. The solution is to swim in, towing your board behind you.

Fig 41 Robby Naish towing his rig in a strong rip after breaking his mast at Ho'okipa.

BEACH STARTING

Note Do not try to beach start your new shortboard until you are sure that you can waterstart well enough to sail back.

Fig 42(a) Once in the water, hold the mast with your windward hand (the one that was holding the footstrap) and the boom with your other hand.

Fig 42(b) Steer the board across the wind on to a beam reach with the rig. Just like sailing a longboard, letting your backhand out and leaning the rig back makes the nose turn into the wind. Pulling in your backhand and tilting the mast towards the front of the board will make it bear off (turn away from the wind). If the water is calm, you can transfer both hands to the boom. In rough water, keeping your fronthand on the mast is steadier.

Fig 43   Dave Kalama.

Fig 42(c)   When everything feels balanced, place your front foot on the centrepoint of the board. Sheet out (luff) the sail just before stepping up.

Fig 42(d)   Sheet in the sail when stepping up. The extra pull gives you something to lean against as you get your balance.

Fig 42(e)   Keep the sail sheeted in and the mast raked forward to avoid heading up into the wind immediately.

Fig 44(a)   Keeping pressure on the inside rail with your back foot, lean back to handle the extra pull in the sail. The rig should be tilted to the outside of the turn. Sinking the tail will make the board turn quicker.

Fig 44(b)   Do not get stuck pointing downwind – keep turning.

Fig 44(c)   Step forward with your back foot and sail clew-first for a moment.

STEERING

At beginners' level, most steering is done with the sail: letting back (clew) out and tilting the rig back to head upwind; sheeting in and leaning the mast forward to bear off. With more speed and smaller boards, the board itself plays a more important role in steering.

FIRST GYBES

Once you are on the water and feeling pleased with yourself, the thought of your first gybe is not totally appealing but you will need to turn around some time. The same method used in turning a longboard will work. Since tacking a small board is difficult, concentrate at first on learning to gybe, i.e. turning the nose of the board away from the wind. Gybing a shortboard takes practice.

Little boards make a wobbly platform at first. It doesn't pay to be overly self-conscious – you will not be the first person to create a spectacle. In fact, watching learners is an acceptable form of entertainment at all the right beaches.

The method is to place your back foot in front of the rear strap and bend at the knees to prepare to turn. Sheeting in the sail and tilting the mast towards the front of the board makes the nose bear off (head downwind).

PUMPING

Pumping is a basic skill. It is a means of accelerating to start planing, and in light winds it will get you home. The action is similar to rowing only you are pulling air instead of water, using your rig as the oar.

Fig 44(d) Grip the mast and release your clew hand from the booms. The sail will swing downwind.

Fig 44(e) Pull the mast towards your shoulder (to windward).

Fig 44(f) Tilt the mast to windward and grip the boom on the new tack, leaning back to absorb the pull of the wind.

Fig 45(a) Robby Naish is towing Jason Polakow (on the surfboard). He leans the rig forward to get a big scoop of air.

Fig 45(b) He then pulls back, as if rowing.

Clew-First Waterstarting

Starting clew first requires more advanced sail control, but is otherwise the same.

(a)

(b)

Figs 46(a)–(f)   The clew-first waterstart. Hold on to the mast while flipping the sail. Christine still has one hand on the mast even as she hooks in her harness.

(c)

(d)

(e)

40

(f)

HARNESS USE

Using a harness allows you to sail longer and use a more powerful sail. The three basic types of harness are described according to where they are worn: these are seat, waist and chest. Seat harnesses are most popular for slalom as they allow you to get your upper body further from the rig while still keeping the rig upright. In waves, sailors need to hook in and out more frequently and, as wave sails are less powerful, most people prefer waist and chest harnesses. A comfortable, well-adjusted harness is an important piece of equipment.

Adjusting Harness Lines

Your lines need to be set up so that the rig will feel balanced when you are hooked in. They should be long enough so that you can sail with your arms almost straight.

Fig 47   Hold the rig with one hand to find its balance point and attach harness lines evenly on either side.

Fig 48   They should be set far enough apart to fit comfortably between your hands when sailing.

Fig 49   For a wave sail, the length of your forearm is a good measure of length to start with. When using a race sail, set the lines slightly longer.

To decide where to place your lines, first stand your rig up in a windy location. Hold on to your boom with one hand to find your rig's balance point. If the sail luffs, your hand is too far forward; too far back and the sail will fall away from you.

Stronger winds will move · the draft in your sail back, so to compensate the lines should be moved back also. Different sails require different placement as well. You may need to readjust your lines once on the water. You should be able to take your hands off.

If you feel more pull on your front hand, move your lines forward; move them back if your rear hand is taking an extra load. They should be set long enough so that you can easily hook in.

Fig 50   To test the setting, hook in and let go with your hands.

Fig 51   With properly adjusted lines you should be able to let go of the booms for a second and keep on sailing.

Hooking In

Sail on a close reach. Pull the rig towards you and swing the line towards your body.

Unhooking

Figs 52(a) and (b)   Take the load off your harness with your arms and let the line fall out of the hook.

(a)

(b)

3
Beyond Basics

Once you can waterstart and use a harness, the real fun begins. This chapter covers flat water manoeuvres from carve gybes to duck tacks and other advanced moves.

ADVANCED STEERING-CARVING

Windsurfing beginners start out by learning how to steer with the sail and balance on the board. A passive stance is sufficient. If you resist the pull of the sail, the board moves. Sailing a shortboard is more athletic. An expert sailor steers with the board more than the sail, pushing on the rails and leaning into the

turn like a waterskier. Carved turns require subtle changes in pressure to keep the board planing. Other moves such as pivot gybes require more aggressive movements.

To turn downwind, the pressure is applied mostly with the rear leg. With your foot either in or out of the footstrap, push down on the leeward rail and lean into the turn.

Pressing your knee to the inside of the turn, keeps your weight over the edge of the board without slowing you down. Speed is required for this to work.

When setting yourself up for a gybe, take your rear foot out of the strap and place it closer to the leeward rail. Lean into the turn gradually. This helps maintain speed

throughout. Applying pressure to your heels makes the board head upwind.

Sail Control

While forces acting on the rails of your board are mostly responsible for changes of direction, the rig must also be controlled. Initially, when bearing off, be prepared to take added strain on your upper body. Moving the rear hand back helps you cope with the load, as does sheeting out the sail and leaning forward into the turn.

A more advanced way of taking pressure off the rig is to oversheet the sail. This works well at high speeds.

Fig 53   Carving.

Once you can waterstart and use a harness, the real fun begins. This chapter covers flat water manoeuvres from carve gybes to duck tacks and other advanced moves.

ADVANCED STEERING-CARVING

Windsurfing beginners start out by learning how to steer with the sail and balance on the board. A passive stance is sufficient. If you resist the pull of the sail, the board moves. Sailing a shortboard is more athletic. An expert sailor steers with the board more than the sail, pushing on the rails and leaning into the

Fig 53   Carving.

turn like a waterskier. Carved turns require subtle changes in pressure to keep the board planing. Other moves such as pivot gybes require more aggressive movements.

To turn downwind, the pressure is applied mostly with the rear leg. With your foot either in or out of the footstrap, push down on the leeward rail and lean into the turn.

Pressing your knee to the inside of the turn, keeps your weight over the edge of the board without slowing you down. Speed is required for this to work.

When setting yourself up for a gybe, take your rear foot out of the strap and place it closer to the leeward rail. Lean into the turn gradually. This helps maintain speed

throughout. Applying pressure to your heels makes the board head upwind.

Sail Control

While forces acting on the rails of your board are mostly responsible for changes of direction, the rig must also be controlled. Initially, when bearing off, be prepared to take added strain on your upper body. Moving the rear hand back helps you cope with the load, as does sheeting out the sail and leaning forward into the turn.

A more advanced way of taking pressure off the rig is to oversheet the sail. This works well at high speeds.

Pivoting

Another method of steering is pivoting. If you snowboard, skateboard, or can do flare gybes on a longboard, you will be familiar with this. Pivoting involves using your back foot to do the pushing and pulling, moving the board's tail beneath you while turning.

A Basic Transition: The Carved Gybe

Experts use many methods to change direction. A carved gybe is a fundamental transition for advancing sailors. This is called a carved gybe because the rails of the board cutting through the water are used for steering.

The key to this manoeuvre is to gybe the sail before changing your feet. Learning to feel comfortable when sailing twisted around is a stepping-stone to many other moves.

Small waves or chop can make carve gybing easier. The push of the wave helps maintain speed through the gybe. For maximum benefit from a wave, start turning early, in the trough. At first you may find yourself ending up on the wrong side of the wave. This means that you started turning too late. .

Spotting a landmark to head towards after gybing can prevent you being stuck pointing downwind. Be sure also to take a look over your shoulder before turning to prevent collisions with other sailors.

Gybe the sail as you pass the half-way mark of your turn. Initially, grab hold of the mast, but, with practice, you can try going from boom to boom directly. To prevent rounding up into the wind, make sure to push your rig forward after gybing, and transfer your weight from the inside to the outside rail.

Fig 54   Pivoting.

47

In Fig 55, Christine Spreiter demonstrates the carve gybe.

Fig 55(h) Catch the booms on the new tack before changing your feet. Do not worry if this feels awkward at first; sailing with your feet facing the wrong way takes getting used to.

Fig 55(g) Concentrate on carving the board and let go of the boom with your back hand to flip the sail.

TIPS

1. Push on the inside rail throughout the turn to keep the board carving.
2. To maintain speed, lean forward into the turn, keeping your back hand pulled in tight, oversheeting the sail, and your front arm straight. Oversheeting stalls the flow of air over the sail, making it easier to handle, and lets you concentrate on carving the board.

Fig 55(e) and (f) When past half-way, use your front hand to grip the mast.

Fig 55(d) Lean forward and apply steady pressure to the inside rail with your rear leg. You will slow down less if the pressure is directed through your knees to the inside of the turn.

Fig 55(i) Shift your feet once you are sailing in the new direction.

Fig 55(j) With practice you will not lose much speed while gybing.

3. Do not lean back or you will slow down. The idea is to carry as much speed through the turn as possible.

4. Wait until past the half-way point before changing hands. The sail will flip quickly, helping you to complete the turn.

Fig 55(a) The sail should be hooked in on a fast reach and you should look ahead to select your line through the turn. It can be helpful to sail around a buoy or other marker.

Fig 55(b) When ready to gybe, move your backhand aft a few centimetres to increase leverage. Place your back foot just in front of its footstrap and unhook your harness.

Fig 55(c) Start carving by pressing your knees towards the inside of the turn. Keeping your front arm straight when going into the turn makes turning smoother.

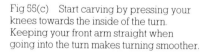

Gybing

Fig 56 shows Ian Boyd gybing.

Fig 56(d)   Sheet the sail in and tilt the mast to windward to bear off on the new tack.

Fig 56(c)   The sail is not flipped until the board is turned almost 180 degrees.

Fig 56(a)–(d)   Ian Boyd showing a variation of the carve gybe, which is useful when you do not wish to lose ground downwind. Were he to apply more pressure to the tail of his board, this would be a pivot gybe.

Fig 56(b)   Ian keeps the sail sheeted in and changes his feet.

Fig 56(a)   The front arm should be straight and applying pressure to the inside rail when going into the turn.

ADVANCED TRANSITIONS: TACKS AND GYBES

Learning to sail a shortboard does not end as soon as you can waterstart and gybe, even without waves. There are many ways to change tacks. These turns are known as transitions. Experts have repertoires of moves to suit each situation. With experience it is possible to keep planing throughout your gybe or spin the board on its tail. Quick tacking and ducking under the sail are other examples. The possibilities are only limited by your skill and imagination.

If you progress to the point of entering contests you will be scored for transitions as well as wave riding and jumping ability. Learning difficult transitions is a great way to get out of the reaching rut. Perhaps you live in a location that does not have 20kn trade winds or consistent mast-high waves. Having learned to waterstart and gybe you might get to the stage where the challenge enjoyed when first learning the sport diminishes.

Not all transitions require planing conditions. You can sail a floaty board, learn the moves, then try them again on windier days. You will soon find out that even sailing in light winds can be challenging.

Ian Boyd, a master of shortboard sailing, helped me enormously by demonstrating many of these advanced moves. In the first 45 minutes of our session he didn't even get wet. This was while going from helicopter tack, to duck gybe, to duck tack and so on. Ian was also a great help in explaining the moves to me; I thank him.

For further study I recommend watching Ian's video *Tricks of the Trade* and following releases, as they become available.

Fig 57   Jason Polakow at Ho'okipa.

Tacking means to change direction with the nose of the board passing through the wind. The word 'tack' can either mean this transition or the direction in which you are sailing, as in port tack or starboard tack. On port tack, your left hand will be nearest the mast, and on starboard your right (if the wind is at your back).

Tacking a shortboard requires good balance and agility. Small boards have little flotation and require speed to keep them on top of the water.

For this reason it is much easier to gybe a shortboard (turning away from the wind) than it is to tack – the opposite, in fact, to longboard sailing.

51

The One-Handed Power Gybe

Learning to gybe one-handed will teach you to have a good feel for the balance point of the sail. This is not a very difficult move to learn. Concentrate on leaning forward into the turn and carving, to avoid stalling half-way through.

Enter the gybe with lots of speed, just as in a normal carved gybe. Speed reduces the pressure on the sail when downwind.

The transition comes when you lean forward into the turn and drop your back hand down off the boom.

The stylish way to complete this move is to use only one hand to control the sail all the way through the gybe on to the new tack.

In Fig 58, Ian Boyd demonstrates this gybe.

TIP

When first learning, put your hand in the water as you flip the rig, as in Fig 58. In Fig 59, Ian uses one hand for the whole gybe.

Fig 58(h) Cross your new fronthand over the old one to catch the boom on the new tack.

Fig 58(g) Pulling the mast to windward helps the sail flip.

Fig 58(f) Flip the sail with your fronthand.

Fig 58(e) Keep your front arm straight.

52

Fig 58(i)   Do not switch your feet until after you have regained power in the sail.

Fig 58(a)   Come in to the gybe at full speed and unhook.

Fig 58(b)   Move your backhand aft.

Fig 58(c)   Oversheet the sail to reduce pull. Concentrate on carving through the turn.

Fig 58(d)   Wait until past downwind before letting go with your backhand and touching the water.

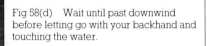

Fig 59(a)   Sail at full speed and unhook your harness when ready. Keeping your hands far apart on the boom as you go into the turn gives you the power needed to carve. Lean forwards into the turn, pressing your knees to the inside.

Fig 59(b)   When you are facing downwind, let go with your clew hand.

Fig 59(c)   Drag your inside hand in the water, while concentrating on keeping the board carving. By sliding the hand remaining on the boom towards the boom's front, pressure is let off the sail.

Fig 59(d)   Let go of the boom while keeping your other hand in the water. Note the tension in Ian's legs – to keep carving you must keep the pressure on the rail.

Fig 59(e)   Catch the sail on the new side with the same hand. The other hand is still in the water.

Fig 59(f)   Finally, grip the boom with both hands. Switch your feet once powered up on the new tack.

The Advanced One-Handed Gybe

This is the ultimate one-handed gybe, not merely touching the water but controlling the sail with one hand all the way through the gybe. Ian Boyd demonstrates this in Fig 59.

Fig 60   Ian Boyd.

Fig 61(a)

(b)

(c)

(d)

A Quick Tack

If a quick tack is completed fast enough, your board will not sink during the transition. This takes practice! Using a floaty board will help you to keep moving through this manoeuvre.

TIP

'It is critical to have a lot of speed. When you are hopping around the nose on a shortboard, it tends to want to stall and sink real fast. You have to be real light on your feet' (Ian Boyd).

▲

Fig 61(a)   From a plane, rake your rig back to turn into the wind. Apply pressure to the windward rail at the same time.

Figs 61(b) and (c)   As the nose of the board comes head to wind, step your front foot forward of the mast.

Fig 61(d)   Straddle the mast while moving around the nose of the board. Hold on to the mast to support the rig as you hop round.

Fig 61(e)   Continue moving your feet on to the new tack and grab the booms.

Fig 61(f)   Catch the sail and tilt the mast forward, driving the nose off the wind with your front foot.

Fig 61(g)   Sail away.

Fig 62(a)

(b)

(c)

(d)

(e)

(f)

(g)

The Nose Tack

Nose tacking is a showy move. Properly executed, the tail comes almost vertically out of the water while the board is spun on its nose.

Enough wind to give support is necessary but you do not need to be planing to complete a nose tack. Using a floaty board at first makes learning this transition easier. However, too large a board makes it difficult to get the tail out of the water.

TIPS

1. When learning you can lie in the water as if waterstarting and turn the tail through the wind with your feet. The sail stays in the same place as you turn the board.
2. Once you have committed yourself to tacking, you will need good balance. Move quickly to avoid sinking the nose too fast or flipping the board.

Fig 62(a)   To begin tacking, rake the rig back and turn into the wind, taking both feet out of the straps. Place your front foot forwards as you come to a stop.

Fig 62(b)   Stepping on the nose causes it to sink and the tail to lift out of the water.

Fig 62(c)   Support your weight on the booms, using the wind to keep you out of the water.

Figs 62(d) and (e)   Pivot the tail towards the wind and settle the tail back into the water.

Fig 62(f)   Having spun the board on to your new tack move your feet to the new side, still holding the sail clew first.

Fig 62(g)   Stand up clew-first, as in a clew-first waterstart.

Fig 62(h)   Flip the sail and sail away.

(e)

(f)

(g)

(h)

Fig 63(a)   Rake back the rig and steer into the wind.

Fig 63(b)   Push hard on the inside rail, continuing to turn, oversheeting the sail.

Fig 63(c)   Turn the nose past head to wind.

Fig 63(d)   Push the rig against the wind, backwinding the sail. Maintain your equilibrium against the push of the wind.

The Traditional Duck Tack

Duck tacking involves ducking under the sail while the nose of the board turns through the wind. The following are two forms of duck tacking. The first, a traditional duck tack, is basically the same as on a longboard, only requiring more balance. This is easier in non-planing conditions. The second is more difficult as you need to keep planing through the turn. A planing duck tack is one of the more difficult moves to execute well. Using a floaty board will help, as will smooth water.

The Planing Duck Tack

Excellent shortboard handling skills are required to pull this off. Ian Boyd makes it look easy – it is not!

Fig 63(e)   Move your hands back on the boom, tilting the mast into the wind. Support the rig with your old forward hand as you duck under then sail.

Fig 63(f)   Reach far forward on the new side with your new forward hand, to catch the boom as close to the mast as possible.

Fig 63(g)   Catch yourself against the wind.

Fig 63(h)   Sail away.

Fig 64(a)   Sail along on a broad reach, planing, and move your back foot next to the mast. Face into the turn (turn around) before ducking under the sail. Concentrate on keeping the board carving.

Fig 64(b)   As you carve the board head to wind, cross your fronthand over your backhand to hold the boom near the end. This will throw the sail forward so you can duck under it.

Fig 64(c)   Now duck under the sail, using your new fronthand to push the sail against the wind.

Fig 64(d)   Let go with your leeward hand and balance the sail back-winded while still continuing to carve through the turn.

Fig 64(e)   Switch your hands to the booms, and keep carving past head to wind!

Fig 64(f)   As the board goes past head to wind, pull the sail on to the new tack and push the nose off the wind with your front foot.

Fig 64(g)   Lean the rig forward to bear off on your new tack and sail away.

(a)

(g)

(b)

TIP
This is a good move to practise on the beach before heading out. The keys to a successful duck tack are learning to perfectly balance the rig in the wind and to keep the board carving through the turn.

(f)

(c)

(d)

(e)

The Pivot (Slam) Gybe

Carving a high-speed gybe is not always possible or practical. If you are sailing in crowded waters or caught in a rocky corner, a pivot gybe is the best way to get around. Also called a scissor or slam gybe, pivot gybing gets you around quickly with the least distance lost to windward. It can be a useful way of rounding a tight mark while slalom or course racing.

The key to pivoting is to move your weight rapidly to the back of your board and push hard on the inside rail. You can either leave your front foot in its strap or jump back with both feet. Using both feet gives a much snappier turn, although control is more difficult.

Whilst speed does make this move more spectacular, it is not essential to the pivot gybe. Speed changes a pivot gybe into a slam gybe.

Move your clew hand back a few inches to increase power and control. Sheet out a little to slow down before turning.

Figs 65(g) and (h)   Flip the sail as if completing a clew-first waterstart.

Fig 65(f)   After turning you will be clew-first on the new tack.

Fig 65(e)   Step your back foot forward to bring down the nose of the board.

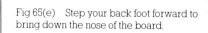

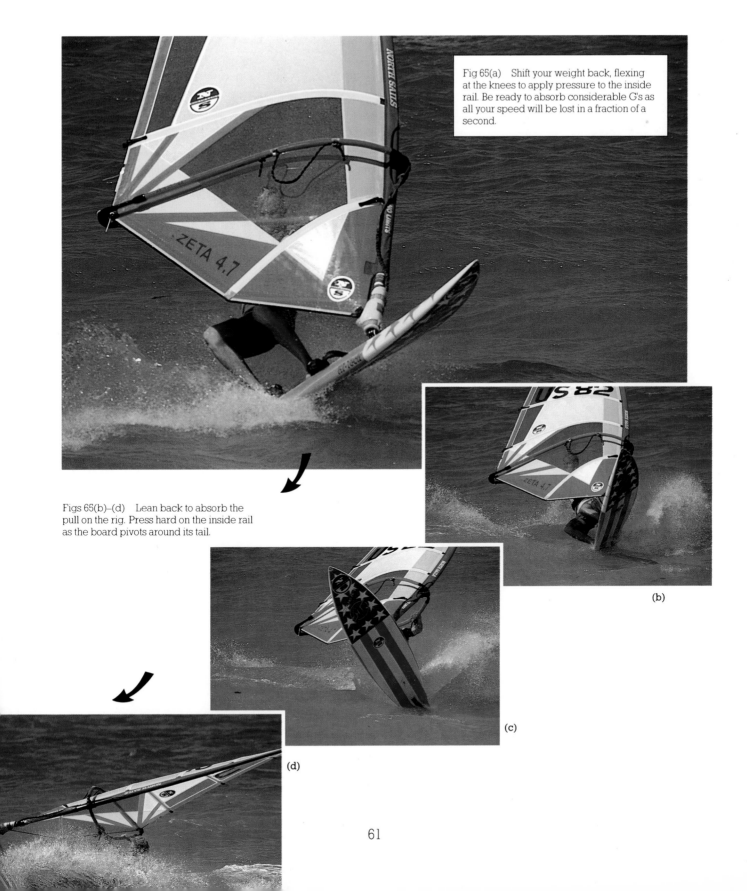

Fig 65(a) Shift your weight back, flexing at the knees to apply pressure to the inside rail. Be ready to absorb considerable G's as all your speed will be lost in a fraction of a second.

Figs 65(b)–(d) Lean back to absorb the pull on the rig. Press hard on the inside rail as the board pivots around its tail.

(b)

(c)

(d)

61

Fig 66(c)   Still holding the boom with one hand, throw the mast forward and duck under the sail, catching it on the new tack with your other hand.

Fig 66(d)   When you have caught it, transfer the new back hand and slide your front hand near to the front of the boom.

Fig 66(e)   Sheet in to sail away.

Fig 66(b)   Instead of flipping the sail normally, let go with your front hand, crossing it over your back hand and using it to grab the boom near the end. Then let go with your back hand. Concentrate on keeping the board carving.

Fig 66(a)   Start your turn as if doing a regular carve gybe. With your back foot out of its strap press hard on the inside rail. Do not try to flip the sail until downwind, when most of the pressure is off your hands. Keep the sail tucked close to your body while carving.

The Duck Gybe

Once you can consistently complete your carve gybes with exit speed almost equal to that upon entry, congratulate yourself; you are now ready to learn duck gybing, i.e. ducking under the sail while gybing.

Speed is necessary to carry you through the turn. Small sails are easier to handle, so don't bother trying if there is not enough wind to plane with a sail of 5.5sq m (59sq ft) or less, preferably one with short booms and a high clew. Flat water and a breeze of 15–18kn are ideal.

TIPS
1.   Speed reduces the apparent wind once downwind, making the transition easier.
2.   Change your feet after flipping the sail, just like in a regular carve gybe.
3.   Releasing your front hand too late makes the sail uncontrollable.
4.   Do not try to sheet in on the new tack before gybing the board.

'Really concentrate on carving the board. Too many people just focus on the hand movement. Once you initiate the carve you have to push hard to follow through with it' (Ian Boyd).

Fig 67(a)   Turn up into the wind and place your front foot just in front of the mast base.

Fig 67(b)   As the nose goes past head to wind, stay on the same side of the sail to finish backwinded.

Fig 67(c)   Maintain your balance on the backwinded side of the sail.

The Helicopter Tack

A helicopter tack involves spinning the sail 360 degrees while tacking the board. This is one of the simpler shortboard moves. First try to learn this tack in light winds on a floaty board.

TIP
'If you don't push the nose around enough, you'll stall. It should be all one fluid motion' (Ian Boyd).

Fig 67(d)   Apply pressure to both the rig and your front foot to steer the nose off the wind.

Fig 67(e)   As your board begins to bear off, push the clew through the wind, moving your feet as well.

Fig 67(f)   Keep spinning the sail, remaining on the windward side.

Fig 67(g)   Release your backhand and use it to catch the mast.

Fig 67(h)   Sheet in, tilting the rig forward to bear off on the new tack.

Sail 360

Spinning the sail through 360 degrees while moving requires some fancy footwork and a good feel for the wind. This is easiest to do in smooth water. Remember, going fast reduces the amount of apparent wind in the sail.

Fig 68(h) Release your backhand to flip the rig.

Fig 68(g) To gybe, sink the tail and lean the mast to windward, pivoting about the tail.

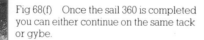

Fig 68(f) Once the sail 360 is completed you can either continue on the same tack or gybe.

Fig 68(e) Move round to the windward side, pushing the clew through the wind.

Fig 68(d) Keep the rig as upright as possible while spinning.

Fig 68(i)   Sheet in and lean the mast forward to sail away on the new tack.

Fig 68(j)   Hook in and sail away. Keep your feet forward of the straps until starting to plane.

TIP

'If you lean the sail over too much the clew can catch. The important thing is to keep the sail upright. If you can do that, it's pretty simple. Then you can keep going or step on the tail and throw it into a gybe' (Ian Boyd).

Fig 68(a)   Bear off downwind to reduce apparent wind as much as possible.

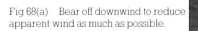

Fig 68(b)   Start spinning the sail.

Fig 68(c)   Follow the sail, placing your back foot next to the mast.

Fig 69   Ian Boyd shows that there are no rules.

TRICKS

Many transitions are tricks but some moves are done without changing tacks. Here are a few:

Figs 70(a) and (b) Supporting your weight on the sail, arch your back and dip your head in the water. Opening your mouth is optional.

The Head Dip

The head dip is an original long-board freestyle trick. It is easy to do, either while moving or just coming out of a water start. French sailors call this move *un shampooing*.

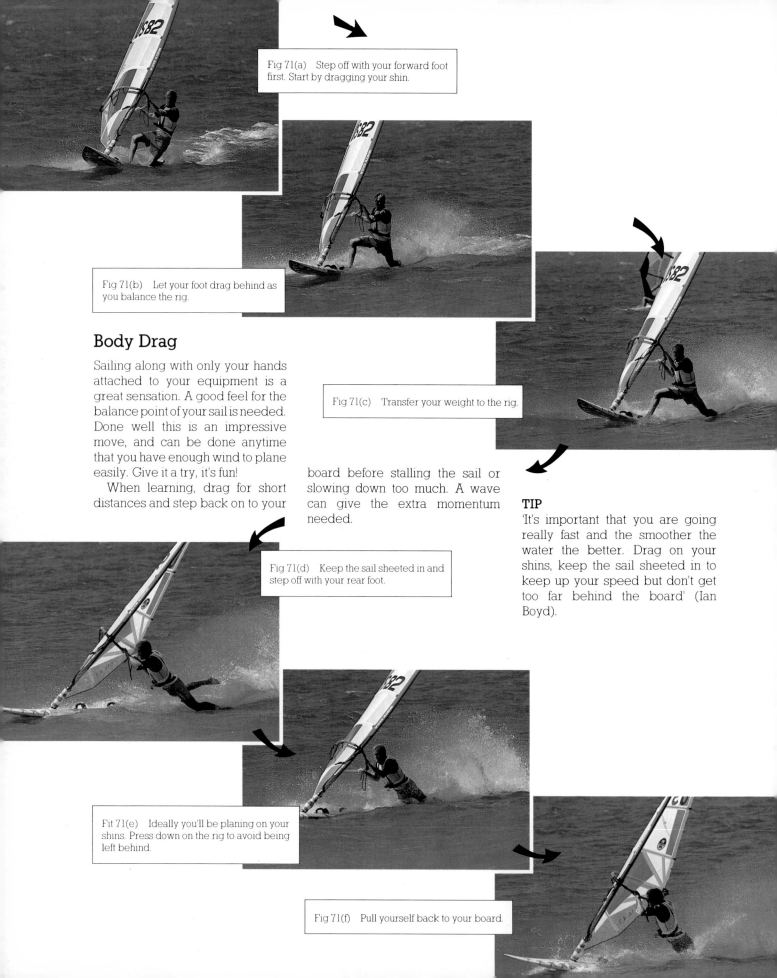

Fig 71(a) Step off with your forward foot first. Start by dragging your shin.

Fig 71(b) Let your foot drag behind as you balance the rig.

Body Drag

Sailing along with only your hands attached to your equipment is a great sensation. A good feel for the balance point of your sail is needed. Done well this is an impressive move, and can be done anytime that you have enough wind to plane easily. Give it a try, it's fun!

When learning, drag for short distances and step back on to your

Fig 71(c) Transfer your weight to the rig.

board before stalling the sail or slowing down too much. A wave can give the extra momentum needed.

Fig 71(d) Keep the sail sheeted in and step off with your rear foot.

TIP

'It's important that you are going really fast and the smoother the water the better. Drag on your shins, keep the sail sheeted in to keep up your speed but don't get too far behind the board' (Ian Boyd).

Fit 71(e) Ideally you'll be planing on your shins. Press down on the rig to avoid being left behind.

Fig 71(f) Pull yourself back to your board.

Fig 71(g) Step back up with your rear foot first.

Fig 71(h) Place your front foot forward of the front footstrap to keep planing.

Fig 71(i) Hook your harness back in.

Fig 71(j) Put your feet back in the straps and keep on going.

4
Waves

Waves are created by either wind or swell. Sailors with experience on lakes will be familiar with wind-generated waves. These travel in the same direction as the wind, although on a lake with a long fetch, sandbars or shallows can force the wind-generated swell to change direction, providing better conditions for wave riding or jumping. When examining a map of an unfamiliar area, look for a point or other piece of land jutting out into the lake to improve the odds of finding good wave-riding conditions during a storm cycle.

Fig 72   Sharing waves is part of the camaraderie of the sport. Sailors have right of way over helicopters, but I wouldn't push your luck.

Ocean swells are the product of storms hundreds or even thousands of miles away. Shallow water slows the bottom of the swell and the top layer carries on, creating the crest of the wave. Ideal wind-surfing conditions occur when a swell arrives during a period of strong cross-shore winds.

River current moving over hidden rocks or boat wakes can also create waves. Major rivers, such as the Columbia, which is between the states of Washington and Oregon in America, produce sizeable waves, particularly in areas where the wind is against the current.

Waves on the ocean change during the day, coming in groups called sets. They ebb and flow with the current and tide and can change in size and shape, sometimes without apparent warning. Storms are cyclic, and variations in intensity, even thousands of miles away and many days before, affect each wave and waveset.

Sailing in waves is a lot of fun. Once you can waterstart a shortboard and feel comfortable launching off the beach, you are ready to try small waves. Some manoeuvres are even easier, especially gybing. In fact, with good timing you will be finishing your turn twice as fast. This takes some getting used to.

Most sailors do not get the chance to sail in waves very often. To gain maximum benefit from your time on

the water, try to sail in the wave zone as much as you can and, when possible, use the power of the wave to get back upwind. Completing your outside transition on a wave will give you more time in the break. For more rides, look for a less crowded spot before heading out.

It is important to be respectful of others on the water, whether surfers or sailors, so everybody gets to have a good time. Sharing waves is part of the camaraderie of the sport.

Success in wave sailing will come from experience and observation. Because you are sailing on a moving mass of water, timing becomes critical. All moves need to be synchronized with the flow of the wave itself. This knowledge is best gained by persevering initially in smaller waves.

When sailing out through a large set in light winds, do not let yourself get caught without power going up the face of a wave. Stall your sail and hang back or gybe to try again when you see a chance to get through. Pick up speed before sailing through the white water.

BASIC WAVE SAILING RULES

1.   Sailors going out have right of way over sailors coming in.
2.   The first sailor on the swell has the right to ride that wave.
3.   If two sailors are on the wave at the same time, the one closest to the peak has right of way.

LAUNCHING

Before heading out, spending time observing the sets gives you a feel for the conditions. Even if the swell is large, you may start to notice sets small enough for you to get through.

Don't be in a hurry; a small set may be followed by the biggest of the day. A close-out set (when the waves break all the way across at the same time) may be impossible to sail through.

Pay attention to the incoming swell and try to time stepping in with the approaching water. Put your board in the water just after the wave hits the beach. Control your rig in the surf with the mast and avoid being caught between the rig and the beach.

Fig 73   When launching, control your rig with the mast. (Sailor Jennifer Auby.)

Fig 74   Do not get caught between your rig and the beach. (Sailor Joe Cool.)

CATCHING A WAVE

Experience, eventually, will enable you to gybe directly on to the steepest part of the wave's face, but at first it is easier to gybe outside the surf break. Gybing outside, the wave will come up beneath you as you sail back in towards the beach.

If you are early on the wave and risk missing a ride, luff your sail to slow down and let the wave pick up beneath you. Start to accelerate while still some distance from the crest or the wave may leave you behind.

Fig 75(a)   As Jason Polakow heads back to the shore, a wave picks up beneath him. He is pumping his sail in the light winds, to catch the swell. (b)   Once on the wave, the apparent wind is coming mostly from in front of Jason because of his speed down the wave.

THE TOP AND BOTTOM TURN

There are two basic moves to master on the wave. These are:

1.   The bottom turn which is a turn made at the bottom of the wave, in the trough.
2.   The top turn which is made at or near the crest of the wave.

Top and bottom turns connect to create a flow along the face of the wave, known as going down the line. Advanced wave sailors will wait until the last possible moment to make their top turn, breaking through the wave crest. This dramatic move is called an off-the-lip and, if the sailor becomes airborne, an aerial off-the-lip.

SURFING FRONTSIDE

Frontside (or fronthand) means that your front is facing the wave. Surfing in this direction takes you downwind as you sail down the line, giving speed for off-the-lips and other spectacular moves.

SURFING BACKSIDE

When going backside (or backhand) the wave is behind you and, at a cross-shore break, you will be gaining ground to windward. In large waves, you may start off going backside to get position on the wave, before turning and going down the line frontside. Riding backside you will have less board speed. Manoeuvres such as hanging five and sailing backwinded (on the wrong side of the sail), are easier – tube riding is even a possibility.

THE BOTTOM TURN

Were you to catch a wave and sail straight down it, you would soon

Fig 76   Robby Naish going down the line.

Fig 77   Robby Seeger surfing backwinded (on the leeward side of the sail).

leave it behind. Turning in the trough to go back up the wave face is a fundamental move, known as a bottom turn. The bottom turn allows the sailor to stay on the wave – the objective of wave riding or surfing.

Sheet in hard and accelerate down the face of the wave, entering the trough at full speed. Pressure the inside rail with your rear foot, driving your knees into the turn, as when carving a gybe. Speed provides needed momentum to climb back up the face of the wave. Keep

your board flowing through the turn, pressing all the way back up for a top turn.

TIPS

1.   Move your hands further apart and lead yourself into the turn with your eyes.
2.   The classic fault at this stage is to sheet in the sail too much. The trick is to place your rear hand further back on the boom, giving more power and balance, then open your sail to the wind to maintain speed. Oversheeting causes you to be backwinded heading back up the wave, and a wipe out is the usual outcome.

OFF-THE-LIP

A high-speed bottom turn sets you up for the off-the-lip. Transfer pressure from your toes to your heels on the way up the wave. A powerful push on the back foot is needed for a quick turn.

TIPS

1.   Bringing hands closer together at the top of the wave increases the 'snap' in your turn and makes handling the sail easier.
2.   At first try to turn early, to avoid dropping over the back and missing the rest of the ride. Timing your top turn to hit the lip every time takes a lot of practice.

Fig 78   Rush Randle bottom turning perfectly – eyes looking ahead, hands wide apart and sail open to the wind.

Fig 79   Rush Randle brings his hands closer together in preparation for a snappy off-the-lip.

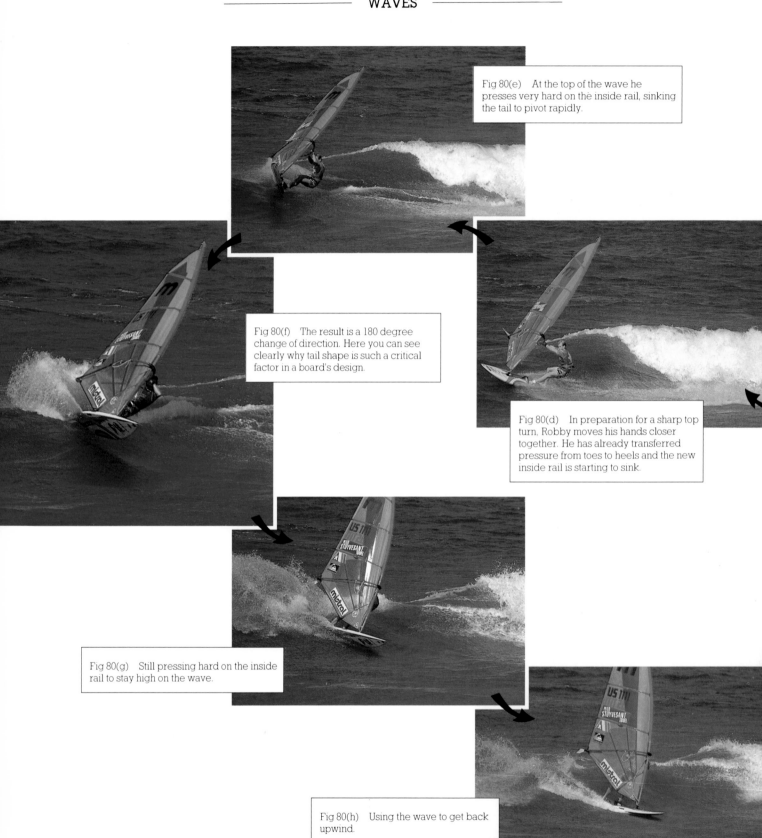

Fig 80(e)   At the top of the wave he presses very hard on the inside rail, sinking the tail to pivot rapidly.

Fig 80(f)   The result is a 180 degree change of direction. Here you can see clearly why tail shape is such a critical factor in a board's design.

Fig 80(d)   In preparation for a sharp top turn, Robby moves his hands closer together. He has already transferred pressure from toes to heels and the new inside rail is starting to sink.

Fig 80(g)   Still pressing hard on the inside rail to stay high on the wave.

Fig 80(h)   Using the wave to get back upwind.

Fig 80(a)   A turn in front of the oncoming lip starts his ride. Notice that Robby is luffing his sail, slowing down to get positioned on the wave.

S-TURNS

In Fig 80 Robby Naish is seen making S-turns along the face of a wave. He starts off surfing backside to gain ground to windward on this small wave.

Fig 80(b)   Pivoting his turn kept him high on the face of the wave. Turning just in front of the lip gives Robby the benefit of the force of the breaking wave, as well as gravity to gain extra speed.

Fig 80(c)   With hands wide apart for power he sinks the inside rail, carving his bottom turn.

Fig 80(1)   A pivot turn to remain on the wave. You can see clearly from the amount of spray that much less speed is generated backside than frontside.

Fig 81(d) Still in the footstraps, Ian doesn't change his feet until safe behind the wave.

Fig 81(a) Ian Boyd planes down the face of the wave.

Fig 81(b) He ducks under the sail . . .

Fig 81(c) . . . and catches the boom on the new side.

Fig 82(a)   Arms and legs extended, Robby Naish pushes down slightly on the tail to get the nose up.

Fig 82(b)   Keeping his front arm straight to avoid rounding up into the wind, he lifts up on the rig for more height.

JUMPING CHOP

A small wave makes getting off the water easier but expert sailors can jump and even do loops on flat water. Weighting or unweighting your board results in rebound from the water, owing to the buoyancy of the board – just like a trampoline. When jumping, think of your board as a mini trampoline. Push hard on the tail and take off on the rebound: the harder you push; the higher you will go.

Fig 82(c)   Tucking the tail up beneath him, Robby prepares for a nose-first landing.

Fig 83 Sheeting in and extending the front leg for more height.

Fig 85 (*Opposite*) A flat jump for distance.
(a) Lift the tail by bending the rear leg.
(b) Extend your legs for landing.

Fig 84 Jennifer Auby landing nose first, sheeting out to let the nose drop.

Hit the chop well powered, with both arms and legs extended. As you leave the water, lift your front leg, tucking your back leg beneath you. Keep your front arm straight, using your back hand to sheet in or out.

Sheeting in gives more height; sheeting out allows further glide but less height. Landing with your legs extended and tensed will help to maintain speed. To land nose first, sheet out slightly and extend your front leg.

It is not necessary to jump every time you go over a wave; by absorbing the wave you can glide smoothly over it.

80

(b)

Fig 86(b)   He leans back and extends his front foot for more altitude . . .

Fig 86(a)   Mark Angulo bears off for a good line up the wave to perform a high floating jump.

JUMPING WAVES

Waves create a more defined ramp, making it possible to get off the water without unweighting your board. Lots of speed makes for big air. Press hard before taking off and you can really start to fly.

With more time in the air, sail control becomes a bigger factor. If

Fig 86(c)   . . . parachutes back down. . . .

Fig 86(d)   . . . and lands behind the wave.

you have gone high (by lifting your front foot), you can use your sail as a parachute to control your descent. Sheeting in blows you downwind. Sheet out to point more upwind.

When coming down from a high jump, a tail-first landing is easier. As you come in for a landing, extend your back leg to absorb the impact, and lean back slightly.

Fig 87(a)   Dave Kalama pushes hard on the tail before take-off.

Fig 87(b)   He leans back on take-off . . .

Fig 87(c)   . . . and uses his sail as a wing.

Fig 88   Mark Angulo 'flying'.

HIGH-WIND SAILING

A day spent sailing in radical conditions may well be an experience you will treasure for the rest of your life. I have one memory in particular. I was woken up in my van early one morning in Corsica by an unusual swaying motion. We were being buffeted by the infamous Mistral, a wind that rockets southward from the French valley of the Rhône.

A peak out of the window exposed my bleary eyes to massive lenticular clouds overhead. Wow! This overpowering sight sent me scurrying back under the covers for further naptime. It is one thing to dream of sailing in incredible winds but quite another to be given the chance.

Bravely venturing out some time later, a neighbour's hand-held anemometer was recording gusts of over 50kn. I was particularly slow that morning. I took pains to rig my smallest sail – 3.5sq m (37.7sq ft) – as tight as I could and checked every line twice, retying every knot.

I spent the most part of this high-wind endeavour out of control. A fact that interfered not at all with the element of thrill. I enjoyed every second! Maybe even those that passed as I head-planted into my sail.

I sailed for as long as I could, taking care to take breaks, eating and regaining my strength before returning for more. And so the day went . . .

Despite the potential hazards of high-wind sailing, common sense and a level head go a long way towards both safety and enjoyment in such conditions. Here are a few things to remember:

TIPS

1. Do not sail farther from land than you are capable of swimming.
2. Even if the water and air are warm, wear at least a shorty wetsuit. Hypothermia saps your strength much faster than any exercise, and strong winds magnify the effect.
3. If the wind is offshore, it will be much stronger further out. Consider having a rescue boat available if the conditions are really severe and make sure somebody on land is keeping an eye on you.

NEVER LEAVE YOUR BOARD

The number one rule for safety at sea is to never leave your board. Brightly coloured wetsuits and sails also make sailors easier to spot from rescue boats and helicopters.

Fig 89   High-wind sailing during a slalom race at Guincho, Portugal.

5
Going Big

When visiting Ho'okipa on a windy day, it is hard to imagine a time when sailors could not do loops and aerial gybes, so commonplace today. Double forward loops and aerial 360's are the moves of the moment and, judging by the action at this world famous beach, there is more to come.

Progress in the last five years is the result of what is best described as a collective learning experience – the snowball effect of one achievement leading to the development

and perfection of another. All in the name of fun.

Technical innovations in both equipment and learning techniques have undeniably played a part. Sails are more powerful and easier to handle and sailors can study photo and video sequences of the very best. However, a sailor's greatest resource at every level of the sport is personal. A desire to seek advancement and the drive to do it. As in other sports, this is the key behind progress.

THE OFF-THE-LIP

With experience in the waves, timing will improve, allowing you to delay your top turn until the last moment. There are a multitude of moves that are initiated at the crest of the wave, from the most basic top turn to an aerial 360. All have in common the need for split-second timing and are best executed in side-shore or side-offshore conditions.

An off-the-lip is a top turn executed at the crest of the wave. Go all the way into the trough on your bottom turn and keep powered up. This is an aggressive manoeuvre.

Fig 90(b) He pushes hard on the inside rail to redirect himself down the face. Keeping the sail flat takes pressure from the wind off the rig. . . .

Fig 90(c) . . . and he glides back down the wave and sets up for the next turn.

Fig 90(a) Ian has timed his bottom turn for good position on the wave and is transferring pressure to his heels in anticipation of hitting the lip.

Fig 91(a)   Jason Polakow carries good speed coming out of his bottom turn and eyes the crest of the wave while riding back up.

Fig 91(b)   He takes off right at the peak, sinking the tail just before lift-off.

Fig 91(c)   In the air, the legs are extended for more height.

Fig 91(d)   The tail is lifted for a low, flat trajectory.

Fig 91(e)   He drops the nose for landing.

THE AERIAL OFF-THE-LIP

To execute an aerial off-the-lip requires even better timing. Your aim is to hit the peak (the most powerful part of the wave) just as it is breaking. From speed comes the power needed to blast through the wave.

Shift your weight to the off-the-lip rail as you hit the crest. Once in the air it is like any other jump.

91

Fig 92(a)   Good air!   (b) Dave Kalama floats over the breaking wave.   (c) Landing in the white water.

WAVE RIDING

As on flat water, the only limits are the sailor's skill and imagination. The following are a few moves performed by some of today's best sailors.

Figs 93(a)–(c)   Jason Polakow gybing off-the-lip.

Fig 94   Robby Naish nose riding. Excellent flexibility and board handling skills make this stylish move possible.

Figs 95(a)–(d)   Ian Boyd carving off-the-
lip and going back down the wave
backwinded. **Note**   Keep the sail close
to the water while turning and concentrate
on carving the board.

(c)

(d)

94

SAILING BACKWINDED

(b)

(a)

(a)
(b)
(c)

TUBE RIDING

Figs 96(a)–(c)   Rush Randle in the tube on
the way to winning the 1990 Aloha classic at
Ho'okipa.

(a)

LAYBACK

Figs 97 (a)–(c)   A layback – a classic
surfing move – by Dave Kalama.

(b)

(c)

Fig 98   Mark Angulo surfing.

THE BOARD SPIN

(a)

(b)

Figs 99(a)–(d)   Robby Naish,
demonstrating typically superb board
handling, spins his board 180 degrees and
surfs tail first. To complete this move, he
can either continue spinning his board
around or stop, step back on the rear of his
board and sail back out.

(c)

(d)

THE JUMP GYBE

An aerial or jump gybe can be done any time that you have enough speed to plane. The easiest set-up is to use a small wave or steep chop to get airborne. This move is also possible in flat water but more difficult.

Dave Kalama demonstrates how to jump gybe on port tack in Fig 100, and Kim Birkenfeld on starboard tack in Fig 101, on the next page.

TIP

'Concentrate on changing your feet as you are ascending. I don't recommend placing both feet in the straps, as you can snap your ankle if you land wrong' (Ian Boyd).

Fig 100   Dave Kalama jump gybing on port tack.

Fig 101(b)   As the board clears the water, use your rear foot to push the tail towards the wind.

Fig 101(c)   Slip the rear foot out of the strap.

Fig 101(a)   Planing conditions, small waves and a cross-shore breeze are ideal learning conditions.

Fig 101(d)   In the air, move your back foot forward of the straps.

Fig 101(e)   Twist your front foot out of its strap to prevent injury.

Fig 101(f)   Get the board beneath you to land in a balanced position.

Fig 101(g)   Land clew first and gybe the sail to sail away on the new tack.

Fig 102(a)   On take-off, the weight should
be completely over the tail.

Fig 102(b)   Begin kicking sideways and to
windward with your back foot, on leaving
the water. Getting the board completely
overhead requires commitment from take-
off.

Fig 102(c)   Twist your upper body around
to face the water while gaining altitude –
being something of a contortionist helps.

Figs 102(d) and (e)   At the apex
of the jump, arch your back and
glide. The sail acts as a wing in
flight.

THE TABLETOP JUMP

Once you are comfortable in the air and able to control nose and tail-first landings, a tabletop is the next jump to work on. This requires altitude rather than distance so the steeper the wave the better.

Since tabletops require a vertical take off, begin placing more weight over the back of your board as you go up the wave. You should be heading up slightly to windward also.

In Fig 102, Bjorn Dunkerbeck demonstrates this manoeuvre.

TIPS

1.   When first learning the tabletop jump, staying inverted for only a short time helps to ensure a successful landing. Work on twisting and untwisting rapidly; upside down hangtime comes with experience.

2.   Keeping an eye on the water throughout the last half of the jump helps to make sure that the board will be underneath you on landing.

Fig 102(e)

Fig 102(f)   Untwist while descending to get the board back underfoot.

Fig 102(g)   Coming in for a landing.

Fig 102(h)   Touchdown.

LOOPING

'Hold on with your hands and let go with your mind.' Good advice from Mike Waltz, Ho'okipa's original windsurfer, on the subject of loops. The first forward loops were only successfully completed in 1987, and the credit for that has generally been given to Cesare Cantagalli. At least he was the first to master the cheese roll – a loop during which the mast is kept parallel to the water and not inverted.

Looping is now a commonplace occurence among top sailors. The limits have even been pushed beyond. For a loop to score well in World Cup competition, the degree of difficulty must be increased, for example, looping with only one hand or delaying the rotation until high in the air. A few sailors, notably Jason Polakow of Australia, have even completed double loops. Though Jason told me that he had broken a lot of boards in doing so.

Now that so many top sailors are spiralling through the sky, there is much interest among improving sailors in learning to loop. Indeed, for those with confidence in the air, learning to loop is a reasonable challenge. For protection in the early stages, consider using a helmet with a face cage. Also, wearing a wetsuit and thickly padded chest harness will soften the impact should you land on your back.

Hesitation and lack of commitment, more than technique, are the biggest factors to overcome when learning to fly. A 20kn cross-shore breeze and steep waves would be ideal for looping. It is more important to have speed than huge waves. In fact, when the surf gets really big, only the very best are willing to risk looping.

Once you can loop in the surf, forward loops are possible anywhere, on flat water or off the lip. Back loops, however, require a wave.

In Fig 104, Robert Teriitehau and Alex Aguera demonstrate a flat water loop.

THE FRONT ROLL

The difference between a roll and a full loop is that while flipping, the mast is kept parallel to the water and does not become inverted as the sailor spins. Front rolls can be done anywhere with chop and steady winds. Aim to launch powered up, with your feet tight in their straps. Moving your rear hand aft increases power and control.

Initiating the roll while still ascending requires less height. To roll, tuck your head forward and sheet in the sail. Commitment is everything here, the flip is similar to diving or trampolining.

Rotation is controlled by the sail, let out the clew on descending to avoid over-rotating. If under-rotating is a problem, keep sheeted in until the board is underneath again.

Opposite

Fig 103(a)   Take-off downwind, lifting the tail and tucking your head and shoulders on lift-off. Sheet in the sail to initiate rotation.

Figs 103(b) and (c)   Stay tucked while rotating, the mast remains parallel to the water.

Fig 103(d)   Sheet out to avoid over-rotating.

Fig 103(e)   A clean landing.

(a)

(b)

(c)

(d)

(e)

Fig 104(a)   Robert taking off on his slalom board.   (b) Alex spinning.   (c) A thickly padded harness can take the sting out of learning.

(a)

Figs 105(a)–(g)   A full forward loop, requiring at least 4.5m (15ft) of air.

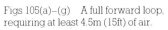

(b)

(c)

Fig 105(h)   With extreme rotation, holding
on can be a problem!

(e)

(f)

(g)

(h)

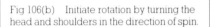

Fig 106(c)   Push the clew through the wind. Keeping the sail flat makes spinning easier.

Fig 106(b)   Initiate rotation by turning the head and shoulders in the direction of spin.

Fig 106(a)   Leave the wave at full speed.

THE BARREL ROLL

A back (or windward) loop should be seen as a natural progression and within the capacity of those who can already do upside-down jumps and are experienced at landing nose first.

To successfully complete a loop, strong initiation is necessary. Sail up the face of the wave at full speed, already pointing the nose to windward on take off. As an aid to rotation, turn your head in the direction of spin – you are pivoting about your back in the air.

Barrel rolls are lower-altitude loops. Steer to windward while ascending the wave and initiate rotation by turning head and shoulders in the direction of spin.

Mark Angulo demonstrates this roll in Fig 106.

Fig 106(d)   Spot landing well before touchdown.

Fig 106(e)   Coming in for a nose-first landing.

Fig 106(f)   Touchdown.

Fig 106(g)   Sail away.

THE BACKWARD LOOP

Jason Polakow demonstrates this form of loop.

Fig 107(a) Lean back on take-off.

Fig 107(b) Extend the front leg for maximum height.

Fig 107(c) Turn your head and shoulders in the direction of the spin to initiate rotation . . .

Fig 107(d) . . . spot landing well in advance to ensure completion.

Fig 107(e) Come in for a controlled nose-first landing.

Fig 107(f) When back on the water, sail away.

THE GU's SCREW,
THE 360 OFF-THE-LIP,
AND THE 360 AERIAL
OFF-THE-LIP

One move leads to the next, out of which comes something completely different. The Gu's screw, the 360 off-the-lip and the aerial 360 off-the-lip are similar manoeuvres, all done after a bottom turn at the crest of the wave.

In a 360 off-the-lip, the board climbs to the crest, then spins completely around to surf back down the same wave, keeping in contact with the water the whole time.

During a Gu's screw, named after Mark Angulo, the 360 is executed in the air and landed behind the wave.

A 360 aerial off-the-lip is the most difficult of these manoeuvres, and the most spectacular. A combination of the two, you take off during the rotation just as the wave closes out, and land back on the face of the same wave.

TIP
The Australian star Jason Polakow says, 'Look for a nice clean bowl. If the wave is right', he demonstrates with curved hand, 'then you'll get one Accordingly, successful completion of these manoeuvres requires ideal conditions, i.e. strong cross or cross-offshore wind and a steeply rising wave face.

Fig 108(c)   Regain the wind in your sail to extend time in the air and float back down. Note that Bjorn's front leg is fully extended and he is redirecting his board with the toes of his rear foot.

Fig 108(e)   Landing.

Fig 108(d)   The perfect completion is to land tail first having turned a full 360 degrees.

The GU's Screw

Bjorn Dunkerbeck demonstrates this manoeuvre.

Fig 108(b)   Success is entirely dependent on committing yourself fully to the move. Keeping the sail flat at the start of the rotation allows you to push it through the wind. Simultaneously extend your front leg and pull your rear leg beneath, as you start to spin.

Fig 108(a)   A classic, fully powered bottom turn will set you up with power going back up the wave. Good carving technique is necessary to turn sharply while not losing any speed.

The 360 Off-The-Lip

The primary difference between the set-up for a 360 off-the-lip and a Gu's screw is that the 360 off-the-lip is executed as the wave breaks. A steep bowl provides the ramp needed to spin, but by hitting the lip as it breaks, the force of the wave provides added momentum, allowing you to land back on the face.

The 360 Aerial Off-The-Lip

With loops commonplace, top sailors need to innovate continually to stay ahead. The following pages illustrate a few examples.

Fig 109(a)   Jason Polakow deep in the kitchen.

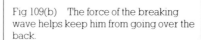

Fig 109(b)   The force of the breaking wave helps keep him from going over the back.

Fig 109(c)   A smooth landing is not assured, as the degree of difficulty of this move is very high.

Fig 110(a)   With impeccable timing, Jason initiates his spin as he goes through the breaking wave. Getting the tail of his board clear of the water qualifies this as an aerial 360.

Fig 110(b)   Landing in the white water is not easy.

Fig 112   A one-handed off-the-lip by Ian
Boyd.

Fig 111 (*Opposite*)   A one-handed jump
by Simon Wilsenach.

117

(c)

(d)

(b)

(a)

Figs 113(a)–(d) A one-legged front
loop by Dave Kalama.

(a) (b) (c) (d)

Figs 114(a)–(h)   A one-handed front loop
by Mark Angulo.

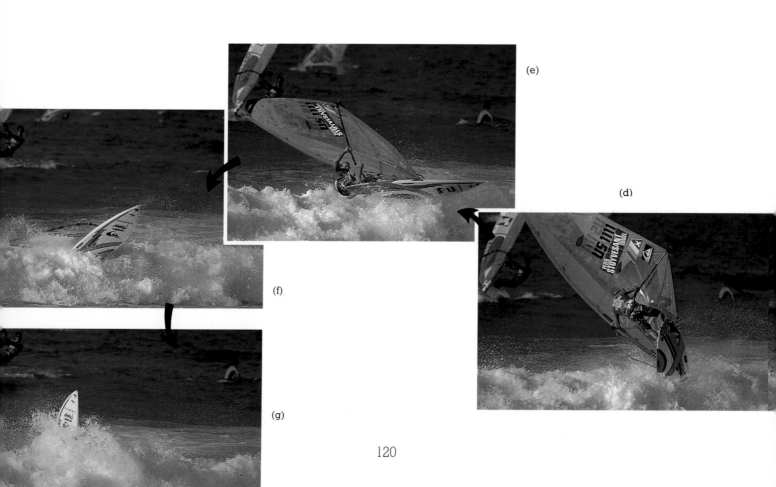

(e)

(d)

(f)

(g)

(f)   (g)   (h)

(b)

(c)

(a)

Figs 115(a)–(g)   A forward off-the-lip by Robby Naish.

121

6
Slalom

Slalom racing has the most spectator appeal of all sailing races. Courses are set with an upwind start so every leg is a fast reach. Unlike course racing where all the sailors race together, slalom is run in heats with only eight to ten racers in each. The heats are over very quickly and the next start sequence begins either when the sailors in front round the first mark, or as they finish. The top four sailors in each heat advance to the following round.

Organizers try to set slalom courses as close to the beach as possible, making it an exciting discipline to watch. When conditions permit, racers will start from the beach, in a Le Mans-type running start. Racers draw their starting position from a hat and line up on the shore. At the starter's signal,

Fig 116 Course racing. The whole fleet starts together.

competitors run into the water and launch together. Otherwise they will start on the water, similarly to course racing but on a shorter starting line, set downwind instead of perpendicular to the wind.

THE LE MANS-TYPE START

The position on the starting line is determined by a draw. In training, practise launching and getting on to a plane as quickly as possible. Usually the first sailor off the beach will be in the lead at the first mark.

Just for fun try carrying your board and rig and running across the beach in a strong wind. The best way to carry your gear is whichever way feels most comfortable. A popular method is to hold the board with your leeward hand

and the mast with your windward, balancing the sail on your head.

Take time getting on board to avoid getting knocked off by a wave and make sure that you are jumping on in deep enough water. Once up, pump your sail like crazy to get planing.

TIP
Getting aboard with one hand on the mast is more secure than holding the boom with both hands. Race anxiety can lead to foolish mistakes, so stay cool.

STARTING ON THE WATER

Slalom boards can easily attain speeds in excess of 25kn. This means that should you be even 2 seconds late, you will already be

Fig 117   The starter's signal.

25m (85ft) behind. (25kn = 12.86m (42.2ft) per second.)

Unlike course racing, the starting line is set parallel with the wind. Sailors closest to the boat end will be upwind of those nearer the pin. As the line is short, starting powered up at the gun is more important than where you are on the line.

Those over-early are out of the race, so an easy to read and set watch is an obvious necessity. Starting well takes a lot of practice; do not wait until the race day to learn.

Fig 118   A good start is extremely important, giving you a chance of an early lead.

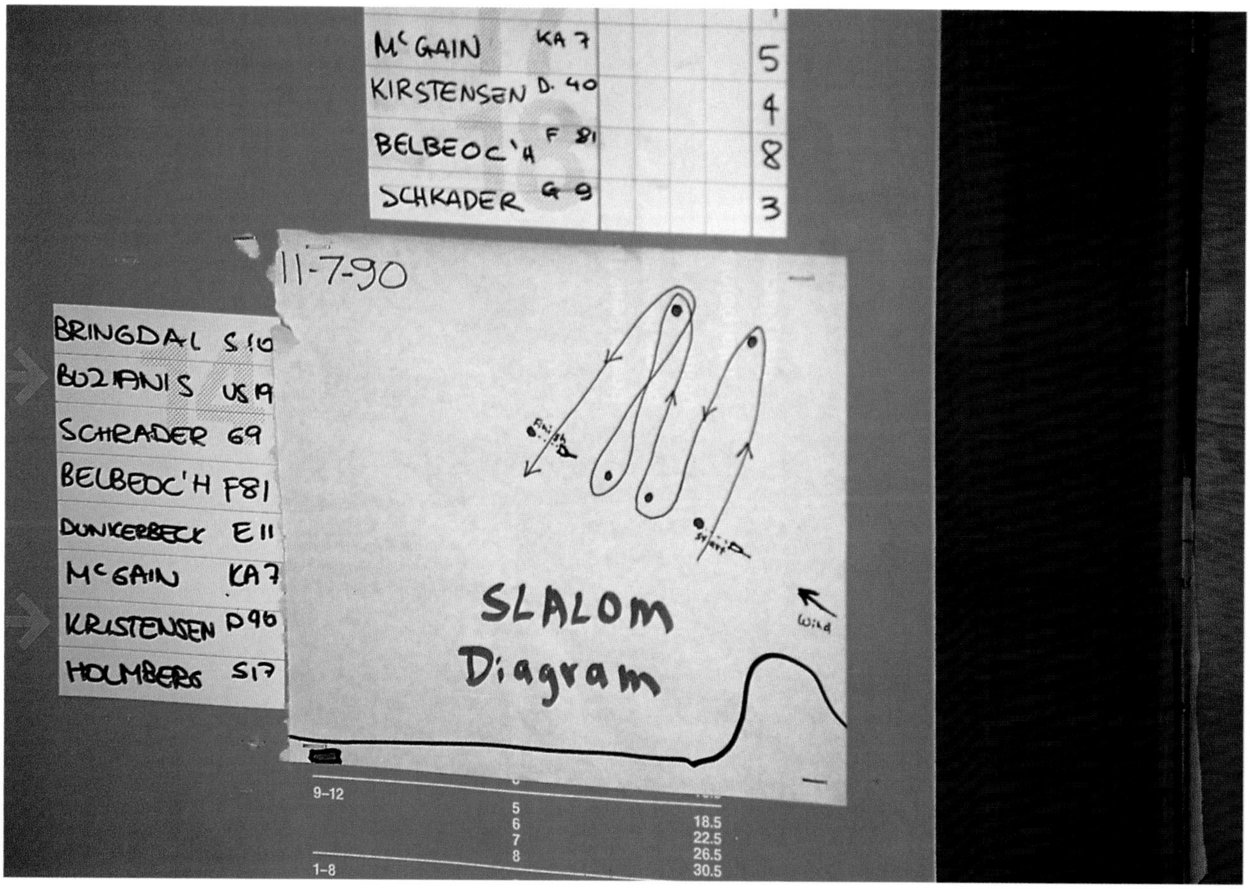
McGAIN KA 7 5
KIRSTENSEN D. 40 4
BELBEOC'H F 81 8
SCHKADER G 9 3
11-7-90
BRINGDAL S 10
BUZIANIS US 19
SCHRADER 69
BELBEOC'H F81
DUNKERBECK E11
McGAIN KA7
KRISTENSEN D96
HOLMBERG S17
SLALOM
Diagram
9–12
1–8
5
6
7
8
18.5
22.5
26.5
30.5

Fig 120 A typical slalom course.

The course is at the discretion of the race director and many variations are possible. There are two basic types.

Generally, in large surf only two marks will be set with the racers rounding them in a figure eight. The inside buoy will be close to the beach and the other outside, beyond the waves. Competitors race around the course two or more times. This type of course is known as 'Ins and Outs', referring to the sailors racing in and out through the surf.

The other type of course, an 'M' course, is set with four buoys, and racers zigzag through them, sometimes including a figure eight around two of the marks. The finishing line will be either between a mark and a boat or, if there is wind inside, on a line between the finishing mark and the judge's stand.

Sometimes the racers come in so fast it is a wonder they can stop before hitting the sand.

Winning a slalom race requires great speed and board handling ability. Slalom races are over very quickly and a single mistake or fall can cost dearly. In preliminary heats, only the first four sailors advance to the next round. As most sailors have similar boat speed, mark-rounding ability can make all the difference.

Fig 119 (*Opposite*) Le Mans-type start.

THE STEP GYBE

In an average round of races with sixty-four sailors, you will have to gybe twenty-five to thirty times and you cannot afford to fall once. Gybing is clearly a critical element in slalom technique. The pressure to perform well is magnified by the need to gybe in the midst of a group of sailors, all trying to beat you round the mark.

The basic slalom gybe is a step gybe. So called because as the sail is gybed you step forward with your back foot to maintain board speed – the object being to keep the board carving and, if possible, planing as you gybe. Stepping keeps the board from rounding up into the wind. It also keeps the nose of the board down, helping you glide through the turn. The best conditions for learning to step gybe are 15–20kn of wind and smooth water. Using a mark to gybe around is also good training. Arrive high above the mark on a broad reach and exit close to the mark.

There are two actions to perform simultaneously: changing your stance and controlling the rig. Learning to keep carving as you change your feet takes practice. The trick is to slide your front foot from its strap, placing it across the board just behind the strap. Then step your back foot forward be-

Fig 121(a)   Unhook your harness and remove your rear foot from its strap.

tween the mast and the front straps. Your feet will then be in the right place to exit the gybe.

As you change your feet, rotate the rig on to the new tack. The rig is laid down close to the water while turning, and then stood up and rotated in a circular motion. To maintain speed, be prepared to take the force of the wind as the sail fills on the new tack.

Mike Dougherty demonstrates the step gybe in Fig 121.

Fig 121(f)   Coming out of the gybe, pump the sail if necessary to be planing again as soon as possible.

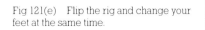

Fig 121(e)   Flip the rig and change your feet at the same time.

Fig 121(b)   Bend your knees, driving them into the turn to start the board carving. Lift up on your front foot (still in the strap) and keep your weight forward by rolling on to your toes.

Fig 121(c)   Move the backhand further aft on the boom for more power and balance. Keep your front arm extended forward, twisting your shoulders into the turn.

Fig 121(d)   Oversheeting as you go into the gybe stalls the sail, making it easier to gybe.

TIP
Looking ahead into the turn helps
take you through it.

(e)

(d)

(c)

(b)

(a)

Figs 122(a)–(e)   Rotating the rig on to the
new tack: A step gybe from a different
viewpoint.

RACING

Racing is not only for the chosen few. There are races for sailors of every standard. Racing is also one of the best ways of improving technique. You will have the chance to watch the best sailors in your region compete, and being forced to manoeuvre in close quarters is great for board handling. The social scene at windsurf races is an added bonus. Going racing is a great way to meet others and have fun.

A knowledge of the sailing rules is important for all competitors. Slalom is different from course racing as all the legs are downwind. For example, the right of way rule has been changed, replacing the port/starboard rule and giving

Fig 123   A protest meeting.

the sailor ahead right of way. However, do not let rules put you off. They are mostly common sense. Should there be protests, they are heard immediately by impartial judges who decide quickly who was in the wrong.

Fig 124   Slalom has a great deal of spectator appeal. This is the crowd at Ho'okipa, Maui during the World Cup.

MARK ROUNDING

Avoiding trouble at congested marks is crucial. Your efforts should be concentrated on rounding as close as possible to the mark and exiting your gybe with speed. If you are rounding the mark by yourself, start your gybe high above the mark when it is downwind and perpendicular to your course.

At a crowded mark you will have the choice of staying clear by going outside, or trying to get through on the inside. Inside, you will have cleaner wind to escape from the pack but one person falling can have a domino effect, trapping the following sailors at the mark.

Fig 125   Avoid trouble at the marks – one sailor falling can have a domino effect.

TIP
Smooth, arcing turns are the fastest. If you are behind some other sailors, stay above their disturbed water and carve across their wake.

Fig 126   Judges on the beach keep an eye out for any infractions; the sailor ahead has right of way.

Fig 127(a)   Britt Dunkerbeck, sail number E7, starts her gybe high and well above the mark.

Fig 127(b)   This enables her to exit close to the mark, maintaining her lead.

Fig 128 Racing through the waves increases the spectacle and thrills of slalom. Jessica Crisp (KA 15) and Lena Kerr (KZ 1) race for the finish.

Fig 129 Robby Naish absorbing a wave.

SURF SLALOM

Some courses will be set with the inside mark near the shore and the outer mark beyond the break; others will only require you to finish in the surf. There are no points to be gained for air time, in fact jumping waves is slower than absorbing them and keeping your board on the water. As you come to the crest, flex at the knees and waist to absorb the wave, much like a ski racer needs to do.

Coming back in to the beach, position yourself by going up or downwind as necessary to get maximum benefit from the swell. Avoid ramming into the back of a wave – being pitched at the finishing line can be heart-breaking.

TRAINING

Training for slalom can be even more fun than racing. Ideally, get together with a friend and train against each other. Having a regular training partner will benefit both of you and it is the best way to test equipment. Even if you do not sail the same speed in all conditions, if you know who is normally the faster, you will find out immediately if a change was for the better.

If you are training by yourself, play mental games. See how many times you can gybe without falling in or set up imaginary starting lines to get a feel for crossing at the gun.

If you have World Cup aspirations you will need to spend a lot of time on the water. Use your time effectively, train seriously and find the toughest competition you can. Most of all, have fun.

EQUIPMENT

Slalom racing is expensive. To be competitive the best equipment possible is necessary. Some World Cup racers travel with six or seven slalom boards and many sails and fins. 12kn of wind is required to hold a World Cup slalom race but there is no maximum limit, so racers must be prepared for anything. The boards are small and light, designed to plane quickly when coming out of a gybe and are very fast.

Slalom sails are also designed for quick acceleration and high top end speed. Whilst racers need as powerful a sail as possible, it must be versatile, with the head twisting off when hit by a gust and the power stable and easy to control. Slalom sails have many battens and camber inducers to lock in their shape.

Most racers wear weight jackets. These are flotation vests containing lead weights or water, sometimes as much as 10kg (22lb). Extra weight enables sailors to use larger sails, which is necessary to be competitive. You should be in top physical condition to contemplate wearing a weight jacket.

Boards

A few years ago, most slalom boards had many channels or concaves on their bottom. These were put there to generate lift, to help sailors get on to a plane. Because more recent sail shapes make planing easier, slalom boards are now shaped for top end speed and control.

The standard bottom shape is flat in the nose going into a vee at the tail. The most critical aspect of shape is the amount of rocker and where it is placed. The front of the board is there for flotation and is only in the water when you are not planing. It is the back of the board that does all the work. Having the right rocker shape is the secret to good design. Boards with a poor rocker line might plane quickly but they reach a maximum speed; other boards become uncontrollable beyond a certain speed.

The best boards are incredibly stiff and yet still light. When tapped, they ring like musical instruments and on the water every ripple is felt. The bottoms of your feet may even hurt the first time out. The object is

Fig 130 The standard bottom shape is flat in the nose, going into a vee in the tail. Pietro Pacitto is the sailor.

to transfer all the energy of the wind into motion, and a flexing board wastes energy. Comfort is secondary. Sailing a well set-up slalom rig for the first time feels like piloting a race car. In strong winds they are both scary and exhilarating.

Fig 131   Bjorn Dunkerbeck.

Fins

Competitive sailors carry a quiver of fins to cover different wind speeds. They will generally use identical-shaped fins in different sizes. The stronger the wind, the smaller the fin. At high speed it is

the fin almost more than any other factor that will have the greatest influence on a board's performance. The search for the perfect fin is not over. Designers are always striving for the ultimate shape.

When choosing which fin to sail with, consider both wind and sea

conditions as well as the course. Most slalom fins are elliptical in plan form. For a downwind course with choppy sea conditions or if you have short legs, you might opt for a slightly smaller fin to make gybing easier. Keep an eye out for wind shifts, I have seen World Cup

sailors unable to lay (make the mark without tacking) the first mark on a 'downwind' slalom course.

It is not easy to tell from looking at two similar fins which one to use. Testing equipment on the water is the only way to know for sure. Sailing with your regular training partner, using similar boards and sails and switching fins, is the best method. Only then will you know if gains made in manoeuvrability will pay off for possible losses in pointing ability or speed. Good preparation and training will pay off on the racecourse.

I spoke with Bernie Brandstaetter, who makes Bjorn Dunkerbeck's fins:

For World Cup, top speed is the main thing. Let's put it this way: if a fin is faster, but more critical for spin outs, the racer must figure out how to not spin out. On the other hand, the elliptical outline is really good against spin out. So I'm not dealing with cutouts, flaps and things for slalom fins, as I would lose top end speed which is not what I want.

Sails

Slalom sails are very powerful wings. To be competitive racers need to be overpowered virtually all the time. To help racers cope with gusts, slalom sails are designed with their centre of effort down low, and the head of the sails made to twist off easily. Looking at the sail on the beach, the leading edge is very full and semi-rigid and the leach is rippled and floppy. These characteristics work to simultaneously create much power and lift with little drag or turbulence.

They are mostly made of monofilm which is a light and stretch-resistant material. The leading

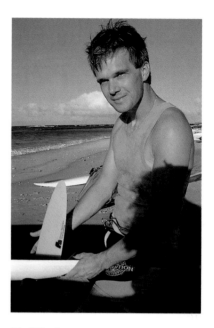

Fig 132   An elliptical foil outline.

Fig 133   A prototype slalom sail.

edge is stretched tight, in a fashion similar to the leading edge of a hang-glider or an old fabric-covered airplane wing. The shape of the foil is supported by many battens, some of which push against a piece called a camber inducer, which connects batten to mast. The camber inducer allows the leading edge of the sail to change as the sail is gybed, something airplane wings and hang-gliders are not asked to do.

Tuning

The board, sail, mast and fin that you select must all work together. In light winds a sailor weighing 75kg (165lb) needs a board approximately 9ft x 22in (2.7m x 56cm) and a 6.3 or 6.7sq m (67 or 72sq ft) sail. For high winds, perhaps a

Fig 135   Well-prepared slalom racer Don Montague, with a seat harness, weight vest and recently wet-sanded board!

Fig 134   Adjusting sails keeps sailors busy on the beach, Robby Naish and Anders Bringdal.

8ft 6in x 20in (2.6m x 51cm) and a 4.5sq m (48sq ft) sail. Most racers will have three complete boards and rigs on the beach and may change only minutes before the start of a race if conditions demand it.

Most slalom sails are set with the luff drum tight and the leech loose and floppy. Familiarity with your equipment and experience are required for optimum tuning.

To keep board and fin as slippery as possible, repair any nicks or dings, and wet-sand them with 400 grit paper (just the bottom of your board, not the deck!).

SLALOM GALLERY ▶

Fig 136 (*Top*)   Robert Teriitehau leading Robby Naish.

Fig 137 (*Bottom*)   Pascal Maka and Roberto Ricci battle it out.

7
Speed

Speed sailing is all about who is the fastest guy on the block. An absolute speed sailing record of 42.91kn was set by the Frenchman Pascal Maka in February of 1990. A windsurfer is now the fastest sailor on the water.

I spoke with Erik Beale, at home in Hawaii, the first windsurfer to crack 35kn and the first sailor of any craft to break through the 40kn barrier. Erik's description of a crash illustrated the forces involved in speed sailing most graphically:

The rocker line of my board at the time was too straight and I got pitched at 40kn. From being fully in control and sailing, I hit the water in not even ²/₁₀ of a second. It was like being hit by a barn door at 50 miles per hour. It hit me so hard that the impact tried to pull my vertebrae through my stomach and out the front, tearing all the muscles in my back, and requiring three months of re-education. They dragged me out of the water and I thought I was paralysed. The rig had disintegrated, everything had broken, the spreader bar of my harness was sheared in half and the webbing was pulled out. The boom was broken in three places, and the mast was broken. The sail was actually okay, as once everything broke the sail just sort of went floppy.

I wondered if speed sailors wore any type of protection for this kind of abuse. Erik told me that he felt the only real protection was flexibility. 'I try to do a lot of stretching and yoga because that is the only thing that will stop you from hurting yourself when you hit. If you are like a piece of rubber then you won't get hurt, but if you're stiff and your muscles are tight, then you tear things, you break things.'

Fig 138   Pascal Maka.

THE HISTORY OF SPEED SAILING

The sport has grown from its beginnings in Weymouth, England, where since 1972 the Royal Yachting Association's annual speed week has attracted an amazing assortment of sailing craft.

The fastest and one of the most exotic boats in those days was Crossbow, a very long thin proa which, after four years of development, reached 31.24kn. It was later replaced by Crossbow II, a staggered biplane catamaran. This boat, owned by Timothy Colman, reached 36.06kn and was retired as the undisputed champion in 1980.

At first, windsurfers were regarded as nothing more than beach toys in the speed sailing world, but people started to take notice when, in 1979, Dutchman Derk Thijs set a record in the 10sq m (108sq ft) class with a then incredible 19.1kn on a modified Windglider (with neither harness nor footstraps!).

WORLD RECORDS

To be official, world records need to be ratified. This means that not only do you have to be the fastest, but you must prove it on an official course in front of trained witnesses. The World Sailing Speed Record Council (WSSRC), affiliated with the International Yacht Racing Union (IYRU) since 1989, provides commissioners for this purpose.

The Council makes and maintains rules for speed sailing. It examines, ratifies and publishes record claims. They also will help and advise organizers of record attempts. A qualified surveyor must measure the course, normally using electronic instruments, to ensure that it is the official 500m (1,640ft) distance.

Setting a world record is an expensive proposition. Not only do you have all the expenses of equipment, travel and accommodation but also course setters, timers and commissioners must be paid for. There is no guarantee of wind on any particular day, either; it may be

Fig 139   Erik Beale holding the RYA, World sailing speed record, Crossbow trophy.

necessary to wait weeks or even months for the right conditions.

Timing World Records

Records were originally timed by hand. Eight timers would simultaneously start their watches in response to the shout of 'NOW!' from an observer in a small boat.

New timing systems, relying on video cameras, are extremely accurate. A VCR, incorporating sophisticated timing devices that generate a clock image on the screen, receives the images from the cameras and a computer calculates all the speeds and sorts them in order. Electronic timing systems, with photo-cells or press buttons to signal starts and finishes, are used as a back-up.

SPEED COURSES

Speed trials can be held anywhere there is windsurfing. To have a chance of making a World Record, a steady wind of at least 40kn is needed and flat water is essential. The ideal spot will have an unobstructed fetch and no current.

Canals

Two excellent courses exist in the south of France, taking advantage of the strong Mistral winds that blow down the Rhône valley. Mistrals can blow at any time of the year, but are more common during the winter months. These courses are at Les Saintes Maries de la Mer, and near

Fig 140   'The Ditch' at Les Saintes Maries de la Mer, France.

Port St. Louis. They are not on the open sea but canals, dredged out of the local argile clay and semi-permanent, needing only to be repaired after storms.

Les Saintes Maries de la Mer (the course known as 'The Ditch') near Arles, has been the site of many records. The narrowness of the channel ensures the flattest possible water for record attempts and the wide flat beach has few obstructions to block the wind. The

canal is about 1,350m (1,480yd) long, 20m (22yd) wide and 1.5m (5ft) deep.

Two canals have been dug at nearby Port St. Louis and this location may have even more potential. It should be noted that this is an industrial area and not pleasant.

The only drawback of canals is that when the wind is blowing from a slightly different direction than the optimum 120–40 degrees, moving the canal is not possible. As you

read this, perhaps a second canal will have been made at Saintes Maries de la Mer, criss-crossing the original, to allow for this.

Fuertaventura, Canary Islands

Noted for strong winds in the summer months this location is famous for speed sailing. Part of the Canary Island chain, Fuertaventura is an island off the north-west coast of Africa. The hot spot for speed contests is Gorriones beach, in the south of the island at Sotavento (appropriately, this means in Spanish, 'where the wind was born'). This may change if planned hotel construction goes ahead, blocking the clear passage of wind across the wide flat beach.

Meanwhile, Gorriones is ideal for speed seekers, the strong offshore winds providing flat water near the beach. Being on the open sea, Gorriones may prove to be of limited use for future records as the water often gets lumpy when the wind is blowing very hard. For speed contests where it is more important to have a good competition than to set an absolute record, it is an excellent location, and there is room for many more sailors than on a canal.

Sandy Point, Australia

A long curving beach, near Melbourne, Sandy Point has great potential as a world class venue, although the curve of the beach is a problem here. A course of 250m (273yd) is easy to set up, but the curving shoreline puts sailors on a 500m (547yd) course a bit further from the beach, and when the wind is blowing more than 40kn it is very choppy even when only 4.5m (15ft) out.

Tarifa, Spain

Located less than 20km (12.4 miles) from Africa, on the southern tip of Spain, Tarifa offers the steadiest winds in Europe. The Straits of Gibraltar act as a natural wind tunnel making this a popular speed venue. The course runs parallel to the beach and is sailed in offshore winds.

Weymouth, England

Although speed contests were a tradition at Weymouth, and many original records were set here, it is no longer used. Britain's national venue for speed sailing is now on a lake at West Kirby, Liverpool.

TECHNIQUE

Eric Beale offers the following advice:

To train effectively you have to be constantly pushing your limits. When racing you have to be fully powered through the lulls and hanging on with your teeth through the gusts, on the limits of blowing up. Then you've got the right amount of power.

When you are out there racing against the clock, you don't have any references. You have to feel what's going on, using both your intuition and your intellect to decide what to use, which sail, board and fin combination, how much weight to put on and, most important, when to sail.

You could be going down the course on a record run and break the record and a sailor at the top of the canal would have waited 45 seconds longer and the wind behind you gets that much better and he'll come down behind you and

break it again. The degree with which you have to tune in on the timing of when to go get's to be surreal.

Starting a Speed Run

When you feel the timing is right for your start, be sure to cross the line at full speed. Avoid following too closely to the sailor in front of you.

Sailing the Course

Remember that the fastest line is not usually straight ahead – bear off in the gusts and head up in the lulls. Look ahead for dark patches on the water and sail around them.

Do not fight the conditions but aim to let your board go with the wind as much as possible. The ability to slide, the French say 'avoir la glisse' is a very subtle, intangible thing and it is a feeling that may take years to acquire and hone.

Keep your board flat on the water. If you get hit by a gust while beam or broad reaching, you might feel the nose lift. This is slow! Press down harder on your front foot, bear off a little but do not sheet out and you will accelerate instead of slowing down.

Stance

The position in which you should be standing depends on your point of sail. Whilst ideally a speed course should be set at 120–140 degrees to the wind, this may not always be possible. You need to learn to be fast on every point of sail.

Close Reaching

When the wind is at an angle of less than 90 degrees, you should have your pelvis parallel with the centreline of your board and most of your weight on your rear foot. Both legs should be straight and your shoulders twisted towards the front.

TIP

If you feel yourself pulling up against the front foot-strap, it is because you have turned your pelvis forward. Turn back towards the centre again and feel your harness hook slide along the harness line as you transfer more of the pressure from the sail to your back foot.

Beam Reaching

With the wind at 90–110 degrees to your board, start to transfer more of your weight to your front foot, still keeping your pelvis parallel to the centre and the sail sheeted in tight and as vertical as possible. Both arms and legs will be almost straight if your harness lines are correctly adjusted.

Spin Out

Your legs must be kept straight to put as much pressure as possible against your fin. If your fin starts to spin out, quickly pull the tail of the board towards you by bending your rear knee. If you continue to have problems with spin out, try changing fins.

Broad Reaching

When broad reaching, your rear leg will be slightly bent and your front leg straight. You should have most of the pressure on your front foot. The sail should still be fully sheeted in, but it will no longer be parallel to the centre of the board. Having too much weight on your rear foot can make the board do a tail-walk and is slow.

Catapults

You can reduce the chances of being catapulted by increasing pressure on your rear foot. This will give you more security but does increase the chance of a spin out. Pulling the rig back more to the rear of the board also helps to prevent being sent flying.

Pressure Control

Speed sailing requires very subtle moves. According to Erik Beale, 'As you go downwind you are driving more and more with your front leg, but the finer points of technique are intangibles. The control is so fine, you're pushing the limit. The closest analogy is piloting a race car'.

Chop

You will only be able to maintain a perfect, rock solid straight-legged, straight-armed stance if the water is very flat, on a speed canal, for example. If you have to deal with some chop, keep both legs slightly bent to absorb the rough spots and keep you flowing over the water.

Waterstarting

As speed boards are so small, you will have to modify your normal waterstarting technique. Place your feet near the balance point of the board. Because the fins are also small they do not generate lateral resistance at low speed, you have to point the board downwind and load the fin once moving.

Fig 141 Waterstarting a speed board.

Fig 142(d)   Pump the sail to get up to speed before trying to load the fin.

Fig 142(c)   Place the front foot forward of the straps.

Fig 142(b)   Keep the sail powered up as you get on.

Fig 142(a)   Push the rig to get the board moving and jump aboard, back foot first, on the centreline between the straps.

Gybing a Speed Board

Speed boards are very narrow and designed for maximum speed, not turning. However, in order to train for speed it is necessary to be able to gybe one.

Beachstarting

The best way to start a speed board off the beach is to leap on with the board already moving. Eric Beale demonstrates in Fig 142.

TRAINING

I think that the best possible training for speed sailing is to sail as often as possible with the biggest, most powerful sail you can handle. You need to learn to handle rough water and strong winds. When you cannot get on the water, do a lot of fitness and strength training.

A strong background in racing will teach you about sailing fast, so I suggest you enter all the races you can. There is a lot to be learned from the best sailors in your region

and I do not recommend specializing in speed sailing without a solid general windsurfing background.

EQUIPMENT

When choosing equipment for speed sailing, the key point to bear in mind is that it should all work together. Follow the advice of R. Buckminster Fuller and think of synergy: 'The whole is greater than the sum of its parts'.

Regarding boards, Erik Beale told me: 'All the design elements are very important – whether it be flex, rocker, vee, rails, the thickness flow – all of these have a major effect on how the thing is going to ride'.

Boards

The object for a board designer is to make a board with the least amount of wetted surface and, consequently, drag. This is achieved by making speed boards extreme-

ly small and narrow. The optimum board is also the lightest, stiffest board possible.

Erik's smallest board was 7ft 7in (2.31m) long by 11in (28cm) at its widest point. The tail – 12in (30.5cm) forward – was 6.5in (16.5cm) wide and the nose (12in back) was 6in (15cm) wide, and nearly 3in (8cm) thick. The deck and bottom of the board were almost parallel from the mast foot to the fin box as were the rails. This design makes that section of the board very stiff. Stiffness reduces deformation of the planing surface if it should hit some chop. Erik was also making boards 8ft x 12in (2.4m x 30.5cm), 8ft 3in x 12in (2.5m x 30.5cm) and a fourth board 8ft 6in x 16in (2.6m x 41cm).

Using a 5m (16.4ft) sail you can bring out a larger speed board, say 2.6m x 40cm (8ft 6in x 16in) when the wind picks up to 20kn. Smaller boards and sails are used in strong winds. The smallest speed sails are about 3.8–4sq m (43sq ft).

Fig 143   The tail of a speed board under construction.

Fig 144   The same board after completion.

Rocker

Similar to slalom boards, the rocker of a speed board is perhaps its most important characteristic. Modern sails are so efficient that only the tail of the board is in the water when you are at full speed. The rocker allows you to rock the board back on its tail as your speed increases, thus reducing wetted surface and, consequently, drag.

The Bottom Shape

Similar to the new slalom boards, speed boards are flat in the nose, going to a vee in the tail. Vee significantly increases control. The flow of water along the bottom diverges from the centreline outwards. This keeps air away from the fin, making it more effective.

Older, concave boards are very efficient at generating lift, riding very high on the surface. They are difficult to control because there is a lot of air travelling back towards the fin.

Sails

Sails are the heart of your speed equipment. They have many battens and camber inducers to lock in their profile. A basic quiver would be three sails – 4, 4.5 and 5sq m

Fig 145   Modern speed equipment, circa 1990.

Fig 146   An old-style speed board, made in two pieces to assist waterstarting. The tail is detached once underway.

(43, 48 and 54sq ft), made of mono-film or other rigid sail material.

Speed sails differ considerably from slalom sails. They have shorter booms to give them a higher aspect ratio. While slalom sails also must be fast, they need to provide good acceleration at the gybe marks.

Speed sails need to generate the most amount of lift possible with no drag. The designer's priorities are top end speed and control.

Even with the computers available to aircraft designers, wings for airplanes are still evolving. Computer design is still in its infancy for sail designers and the feedback comes from real 'seat of the pants' test pilots. The golden age of speed may be yet to come.

This is what Erik has to say:

Control is very important. If you have a very powerful foil section but one that stalls easily, with twitchy lift characteristics, it may be very *fast over 50m [55yd] but we have to average our speed over 500m [550yd]. The ideal sail design needs to be incredibly adaptive. It has to be able to react instantly to a very wide range of wind speeds and angles of attack because all those things change constantly. The foil has to operate in a very turbulated environment, ever changing. You are very close to the ground so you are getting irregularities in speed and wind direction, even where it might be lifting slightly or descending slightly.*

Wing Sails

A few years ago sailors tried racing with so called wing sails, rigid foils made of carbon fibre. They found them to be very fast but too sensitive to sail easily. As soon as their boards hit any sort of chop, the wing would shake off the laminar flow of air from the leeward side, switching off the power to the sail.

SAIL TUNING

Try setting up your sail as you would for slalom. The downhaul controls leech tension. For broad reaching, the sail should be set so that leech just starts to be loose. This helps you to bleed off excess power in gusts, and keeps the centre of effort down low.

The tack strap at the bottom of the sail controls the bottom of the foil. Loosening it off will let wind bleed off but too much and you will be losing power. Setting the tack strap too tight will cause the foot to stall.

The correct adjustments let you sail fully powered up in the lulls and bleed off excess power in the gusts.

CLOSING THE GAP

Adjust your mast foot so that the foot of the sail sets parallel and close to the deck of your board. If just the back of your sail touches the board, move your mast foot back. If the back of the sail is too high off the board, move the mast foot forward.

Rig Adjustment

It is very important that you are in tune with your equipment – foot-

Fig 147   Equipped for speed: a narrow speed board, a multi-battened sail, a seat harness and a weight jacket.

Fig 148   A tack adjuster.

straps, harness, harness lines, boom and sail must all be adjusted correctly.

Booms

Erik told me: 'According to Bjorn Dunkerbeck, "Where you put the boom on should be irrespective of what's comfortable. You put it on there to make the sail twist a certain way." You might deliberately sail with your boom lower to make the sail more flexible, to have more dynamic twist. If you set your booms too high it will be difficult to water start.'

Fins

Speed fins are raked back slightly more than slalom fins. The purpose of the rake is to prevent the leading edge from going past vertical (making the foil ineffective) should you

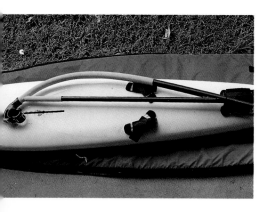

Fig 149   An asymmetrical boom for record attempts.

hit some chop. Erik's fins ranged in depth from 190–260mm (7½–10in) and he had different sizes every 15mm (⁹⁄₁₆in) in between.

Erik said this:

Fins are the reflection of the sail

underwater. Because water is so much denser than air, the fin needs to be considerably smaller than the sail. Both the size of the fin and its foil section have an effect.

A point to consider is the angle of attack of the fin, its path through the water. The ideal angle is about 4 degrees. A very thin foil section is theoretically faster but is going to need a greater angle of attack to generate lift, which can create more drag.

Most of my fins are around 10 per cent foils, as are my sails. In 1988, most people were using foils of about 12 per cent. If you use a narrower foil it has to be slightly deeper. The thickest point is 50 per cent back. Having both the leading and trailing edges curving – an elliptical shape – allows you to foil a better fin. The tip vortex's are bled off, effectively generating less turbulence. I make my fins as rigid as possible through the bottom two-thirds; if the tip is slightly flexible it might give you a little more user friendliness.

Tuttle boxes are the most effective method of attaching fins to a board. Do not use too small a fin at first, 23–25cm (9–10in) of depth would be a good size to start with. If the wind is really strong you can use smaller fins, 18–20cm (7–8in) long, but remember that too small a fin will make waterstarting and sailing back upwind more difficult.

Some racers use asymmetrical fins. Pascal Maka used a 220mm (8in) asymmetrical Curtis fin when he set the record at 42.91kn. The choice is ultimately up to the racer. Try a variety of fins and see what works best for you.

Harnesses

A seat harness is essential. It will

Fig 150   A speed fin.

help keep your centre of gravity low, giving you more power than a waist or chest harness. Harness lines can be set closer together than on a slalom sail as speed sails have shorter booms. When setting harness lines, start with them forward to make a catapult less likely. Then gradually move them back until you find the most balanced position.

TIPS

1. If control is a problem, try lowering your booms or using a different fin. If you feel that your equipment is not adjusted properly, do something about it, go back to the beach and fix it. Use a waterproof marker to mark the ideal settings for your booms and mast base.

2. Avoid setting your sail too full, because the apparent wind is so far forward a flatter sail is required. A fuller sail will give you better acceleration but at maximum speed will create drag. Speed sails are designed to be rigged with a lot of downhaul tension, this locks in the draft and makes the sail more predictable and easier to handle in strong winds.

Weight Jackets

Like slalom racers, many speed sailors use weight jackets to help them hold down a larger sail size. These use lead or water for weight, although lead is more aerodynamic. Make sure that your jacket still offers positive buoyancy.

ORGANIZING A SPEED TRIAL

It is complicated to organize a World Record attempt, and requires the help of the WSSRC, but running a speed trial event for fun is well within the capabilities of small windsurfing clubs or other organizations. The ideal location would be a sandy spit, with unobstructed wind where transit marks can be easily set up.

Timing

The simplest method is to set up a speed trap with a borrowed radar gun. However, these can be difficult to time accurately with. Another way to set up a small trial is to find a measured distance on the water and time sailors over the distance with a stop-watch. If you do not have a surveyor's transit handy for measuring the distance between two buoys, check your local chart. You may find two conveniently located channel markers or other fixed buoys. Or perhaps you could use land-based transits, along the harbour wall or beach.

Short Courses

It is not necessary for a course to be the official length of 500m (547yd) for sailors to have fun. A shorter course of 250m (273yd) will be easier to organize and provide sailors with more runs. Take note: it only takes 24.33 seconds to cover 500m at 40kn. With fast sailors, it will be difficult to time accurately on a course of less than 250m using stop-watches.

Course Layout

Your course need not be set at the optimum angle of 120–140 degrees off the wind, but sailors will achieve higher speeds at that angle. If you are organizing a contest where less experienced sailors may be taking part, consider setting a course closer to 90 degrees to the wind. Sailors will not be travelling at their highest possible speed but you will be less likely to lose them downwind, unable to return in time for another run.

Try to set up your speed course in an area that is free of obstructions, both on the water and on the land. A clean run-up for the wind will give a fairer chance to all sailors. At the Sotavento course, the wind has a fetch of more than 1km (0.62 miles) before blowing offshore, which is one of the reasons why it is such a good location for speed trials.

Safety

Offshore winds are most conducive to speed, as they provide the flattest water. Remember to have some kind of rescue boat available to help sailors who break down. In many areas the spring and fall equinoxes provide the strongest winds, but do not forget wind chill as a factor – hypothermia is a real threat in these conditions.

Apparent Wind

The wind felt by your sail is called apparent wind, it is a combination of the speed of the true wind and the wind that you create from your motion through the water. It is this apparent wind that makes it possible to sail faster than the true wind. (*See also* page 24.)

The record at the time this book was written was over 40kn. In February 1990 Pascal Maka of France went 42.91 knots in the canal at Les Saintes Maries de la Mer, France. This speed is equal to 79.47kph (49.4mph), or 22.075m (42yd) per second. Five hundred metres (547yd) – the minimum length for an official speed course – are covered in 22.65 seconds. Who knows when somebody will sail 50kn? You can bet that it will take a lot of wind and a very well prepared sailor.

8
Travel

Whether just a day trip or a six-month voyage, windsurfing involves travel for almost everybody who sails. Few can boast perfect sailing conditions in their backyard.

There are many centres around the world that are completely set up for high-performance sailing, some offering accommodation and instruction as well as equipment for a complete package. Centres such as these offer a choice of boards and sails suitable for local conditions. Windsurfing package holidays are great for those just getting into shortboard sailing. Before booking a holiday at a particular centre, check that the equipment available is of recent design and in sufficient quantity to go around.

An alternative to basing your holiday at a windsurfing resort is to visit an area that has top-quality rental gear available. Experienced

sailors, who do not need an instructor or rescue boat around, benefit most from this choice.

It gives you the chance to explore different beaches and surf spots too. For example, both Maui, Hawaii and the Columbia River Gorge in Oregon/Washington, USA

Fig 152   A windsurfing shop in Maui.

have inexhaustible supplies of excellent equipment for rent. In order to cater for such a large group of transient sailors, both locations have shops offering great deals on used equipment, making both of these places a good choice for sailors looking to buy equipment at bargain prices. Some stores also buy back equipment or sell on commission. Even better deals are often found at the beach where sailors returning to Europe unload unwanted gear the day before leaving.

Purchasing boards and sails may be a better deal if your vacation is longer than a couple of weeks. Buying the best new equipment available is not a problem in Maui or the Gorge. In fact you will be spoiled for choice. That is if you are looking for a shortboard; about the only longboards you are likely to see are in the rental shops or on the roofs of racers passing through.

An important point to be aware of when travelling is that windsurf-

ing equipment is not standardized throughout the world. If you are travelling with your own, make sure to bring along spares of anything unique to your rig, especially a spare mast base and fin screws/ plates. Failure to do so can spoil the fun and involve unplanned spending.

A SHORT GUIDE TO SOME POPULAR DESTINATIONS

Mother Nature is at best unpredictable but you can improve the odds of finding good windsurfing by visiting areas at the time of year that they are most likely to have wind. You will not be able to learn to waterstart and sail a shortboard if the wind is blowing less than 15– 18kn, which is about force 5.

Maui, Hawaii

Famous world-wide for wind and surf, Maui is also an excellent loca-

Fig 151   Cesare Cantagalli sailing in Hawaii.

Fig 153   World Cup racer, Anders Bringdal, on the road.

tion for improving sailors. The best winds occur during summer – May through August – although the surf is generally small at this time of year. The biggest swells hit the Hawaiian islands in the winter but the trades are less reliable then. For a chance of wind and waves, the best months are May and October.

The Caribbean

In the Caribbean, excellent sailing can be found on many of the islands. Trade winds blow here all year round but are most consistent in April through July. The Dominican Republic and Puerto Rico are both developing very good reputations and Puerto Rico is noted for being inexpensive.

ARUBA
The closest island to Venezuela, Aruba is noted for flat water sailing and strong offshore winds, especially during June and July. Most of the year has wind but September through November are the least reliable months.

BARBADOS
Further east in the Caribbean, Barbados has strong wind from December through March and excellent wave sailing too.

CANCUN, MEXICO
In the Western Caribbean, Cancun is also windiest December through March.

PUERTO RICO
This island is being discovered by more sailors every year. It is still inexpensive and has some of the best wave-sailing conditions in the Caribbean. Wind is consistent in the summer with small waves. Winter sees the best waves but less consistent wind.

Baja, Mexico

Los Barriles and La Paz, Mexico, located on the southern tip of the Baja peninsula on the Sea of Cortez, are becoming increasingly popular with shortboard sailors from the US. The area is not yet well known to European sailors. There are a number of beaches to sail from and

good facilities available in some of the specialized windsurfing resorts. The sailing season runs from November to March with the months December to February being most reliable for wind.

The Mediterranean

Some of the best spots for shortboard sailing in the Mediterranean Sea are Crete, northern Sardinia, southern Corsica and Tarifa. In the summertime excellent sailing can be found in the eastern Mediterranean on Crete and other surrounding isles. The central Med, northern Sardinia and southern Corsica also offer consistent winds and warm clean water. Further west, Tarifa is famous for strong wind but is to be avoided in July and especially August due to the crowds. The recommended months are May, June and September but the wind can blow at any time.

The Canaries

Located in the Atlantic Ocean off the coast of Africa, the Canary Islands are very popular with European sailors. It is windiest in the summertime when both excellent waves, high wind, and flat water sailing can be found there. Like Tarifa, you can expect to sail with sails as small as 3.5sq m (37.7sq ft) or even smaller, for at least part of the time during the summer months – June, July and August.

SAILING KIT

How much to bring is a personal choice. If you will be renting, all you need is your own wetsuit, harness and perhaps sailing shoes (in case your rental board is slippery or if you are launching in rocky areas). A World Cup sailor may travel with up to 275kg (600lb) of gear, with as many as twelve boards.

If travelling light you can get by with one board, a couple of sails, a two-piece mast and a set of booms. All your luggage together could weigh less than 18kg (40lb).

A TRAVEL CHECK-LIST

● Passport, valid driver's licence, credit card, visa (if necessary)
● Sunscreen, sun-glasses, cap, sunburn cream, camera
● Handbook with local information
● Board
● Two or three sails of sizes common at your destination, two-piece mast
● Adjustable booms
● Spare fin, fin repair tab, fin screws and fin screw plates
● Spare line
● Small repair kit, duct tape
● Wetsuit (shorty or vest only if you are going to the tropics)
● Soft roof rack to fit on any car (few car rental agencies can provide racks)
● Flashlight
● Pocket calculator

A First-Aid Kit

● Neosporin, peroxide for cleaning cuts and preventing infection
● Cloth band-aids (stick better than plastic)
● Extra-strength aspirin, antihistamines
● Lomotil and Swim ear
● A meat tenderizer for stringray and jellyfish sting (apply gently, don't rub, and soak in hot water)

Fig 154   A well-equipped van.

● Good tweezers, sharp scissors, and an eye-wash kit

TRAVELLING CLOSER TO HOME

Racks

Use a sturdy rack, firmly attached to your car. Pad it to protect your board from damage, especially if you have a custom fibreglass board, as they are not generally as durable as production boards. Care should also be given in your choice of tie downs – use webbing straps or similar. A padded board bag provides additional protection from knocks and ultraviolet rays, which break down and weaken fibreglass. Mast/rack clips are available to make life easier. To discourage theft, get locks for your racks and board. When travelling with more than two boards you will need to stack them. Place solid foam pads between the boards. Tower racks, using a centre post with bars com-

ing out to the side, permit you to pull out whichever board you require without having to undo the whole stack.

Fig 155   Racks should be well padded.

Fig 156   Flying.

FLYING

The logistics of travelling with a pile of sailing equipment may at first seem daunting. Taking time for a little advance planning can prevent unwanted adventure. Your equipment should be in well-padded bags, as baggage handlers are usually hired for brawn rather than finesse. Be sure to label all baggage clearly inside and out.

Many airlines permit you to travel with two pieces of hold baggage and one carry-on piece. This means that you are able to travel with board and quiver bag to-

Fig 157   The beach at Ho'okipa.

gether as one piece and one large carry-all. Excess charges often seem to be at the whim of the check-in person, so a little luck is needed.

Arrive at the airport early; you will need the extra time to cart your gear about and it is more likely that your baggage will arrive at the same time as yourself. Bring a soft

roof-rack. They are easy to pack and fit most cars.

Jet Lag

If you have just travelled half-way around the world to go sailing, the chances are that your body will be a little bit out of sync with your surroundings. You may not feel like

Fig 158   Uncrowded sailing down the coast on Maui.

slashing the waves for a few days if you suffer badly. Drinking plenty of water on the flight can help. One of the best ways of overcoming jet lag is to change to local sleep time as soon as you arrive, even if you need sleeping pills the first couple of nights.

9
Sailors' Health

SUNBURN

The sun's potential to damage our skin is increasing with the depletion of the ozone layer. Sunburn is an obvious hazard in most windsurfing locations but we can all admit to neglecting to properly protect ourselves at some time.

Often it takes an annual dose of sunburn before a more sensible attitude and the appropriate habits are adopted. Unfortunately, that can be very painful. It may lead to nausea, dehydration and chills, not to mention the boredom of a day or two spent indoors off the water.

Bear this in mind the next time you hit the beach. Cover up all exposed skin with a broad-spectrum waterproof sunscreen regularly throughout the day. Do not underestimate the danger on hazy days, when the risk of sunburn is often increased, and be aware that being on the water makes you twice as vulnerable as on land.

Professional sailors take the sun seriously. Preventing sunburn means preventing the growth of skin cancer also, which is a risk to all of us. Some prominent sailors have already fallen victim to this terrible disease.

Treatment for Sunburn

1. Hydrate – drink lots of fluids.
2. Take a cool shower.
3. Cover yourself with gel, not oil. Aloe vera is recommended.
4. Rest, stay indoors and wear lightweight clothes to prevent a chill.

SKIN CANCER

Cancer, the big C. The sun presents a big risk to all who spend time in it. This has been reflected by an increase in the incidence of skin cancers, particularly malignant melanomas, over the last twenty years. The first signs of malignant melanomas are moles which change colour (usually becoming red or black). They may become itchy. Don't ignore these warning signs, as skin cancers are the most easily treated form of cancer if diagnosed early.

Like all cancers, malignant melanomas are potentially fatal if ignored. Sunburn is the most likely trigger of skin cancer. Fair-haired people are the more vulnerable, but all sailors are at risk, as the intensity of the sun is magnified by the water.

INJURIES

Windsurfing provides a great opportunity to enjoy physical exertion in the great outdoors. It is up to us to ensure there is a minimal risk of injury.

Windsurfing is one of the safest thrill sports there is. Just be aware of yourself and the surroundings and it is unlikely that you will suffer anything worse than the occasional bump.

Bumps and Bruises

To treat a bruise, apply ice to reduce swelling. Arnica cream or lotion applied to the bruised skin works very well, helping reduce both the pain and the bruising. Arnica should not be used on open wounds.

Cuts and Scrapes

The occasional scrape is not normally a problem if you wash it and keep it clean. Special care should be taken in the tropics. Even small

Fig 159   Accidents can happen.

scrapes can take months to heal. Be especially wary of coral cuts. To avoid infection, wash scrapes thoroughly and use a strong topical antiseptic – Betadine works well. If a cut is deep, see a doctor, and it is wise to stay out of the water for a few days. Sailors in warmer tropical climes should apply waterproof dressing and tape until the wounds are sealed over.

Over-Use Injuries

Sailing many hours a week can lead to over-use injuries. Using too large or too small a diameter boom can trigger problems for some people. These include carpal tunnel syndrome and tennis elbow. Rest is normally recommended – frustrating but necessary.

Carpal tunnel syndrome results from the main nerve to the hand being pinched at the wrist. Symptoms include a tingling sensation in the middle three finger tips, an aching on the inside of the wrist and a loss of grip strength. Most people are cured by wearing a special splint for a month. Minor surgery will relieve the pressure on the nerve in more severe cases.

Pain on the outside of the elbow is a symptom of tennis elbow. This condition is common among carpenters and others who work with their hands. It is caused by repetitive rotation of the forearm. A brace worn over the muscle next to the elbow can allow you to keep sailing or playing tennis and prevent the condition worsening.

Prevention: the Best Medicine

Most big problems start out as little ones. Listen to your body. Is it aching because this is the first exercise you have had in a month or is a nagging discomfort getting worse? Sometimes the solution is to change the boom diameter or your grip. Stretching and muscle training also help prevent injury.

Correct rigging makes sailing easier and removes unneeded stress. Use harness lines of the right length. If you are still sore, consider changing harness type or hook height. Most windsurfing-related back problems can be prevented by building up muscle strength in the lower back.

Jellyfish Stings

Portuguese man o' war and other jellyfish – little blobs of jelly-like protein floating around the ocean – don't have many ways of protecting themselves. I am not a marine biologist, so I cannot offer technical details, but from experience I can tell you that the poison emitted from their tentacles is very effective.

Jellyfish drift with the wind and current. Man o' wars (or blue-

Fig 160   A Portuguese man o' war.

bottles) are little blue bubbles which catch the wind and trail tentacles up to 6m (20ft) long. They don't usually infest a beach for long but you should keep an eye out for them before launching. If they are about, you can usually spot a few of them at the water's edge.

Wearing a wetsuit is the only protection. If you should fall among them, a mast pad is a useful tool for removing the poisonous tentacles from your rig.

SYMPTOMS
Pain on contact is almost instantaneous and can last for a few hours. Sometimes welts or raised flesh are experienced and these can last for a few days. Some people are more sensitive than others; those most allergic can experience severe shock and may need help – a good reason not to sail alone.

TREATMENT
Urine is very effective in helping reduce the sting. Other acids such as vinegar can help too. Another

remedy is to apply unspiced meat tenderizer, made into a paste with warm water. It helps in removing the poison from your system. Avoid touching the affected area.

HAZARDS

Different hazards exist in each region. When new to an area, don't rely on luck; check with the natives before heading out and take a good look around yourself. For example, in the Columbia Gorge, small tugboats pull barges which follow hundreds of metres behind. It is easy to assume that the two are unconnected, as the cables are submerged owing to their length. However, the captain must plan kilometres ahead before stopping and should you fall he would be unable to take avoiding action.

Broken glass is a more common problem, even at the prettiest beaches. I once cut my foot very badly, stepping on to a broken bottle while launching.

10
Photo Gallery

Jennifer Auby

Dave Kalama

Rush Randle

Robert Teriitehau

Nigel Howell

Robby Naish

Paul Bryan

Appendices

1 A FOUR-LANGUAGE DICTIONARY FOR SAILORS

When travelling the world, some of the following words may come in handy at the beach or when trying to read the weather map.

ENGLISH	GERMAN	FRENCH	SPANISH
direction	richtung	direction	direccion
north	Nord	nord	norte
south	Sud	sud	sur
east	Ost	est	este
west	West	ouest	oeste
sea	Meer	mer	mar
coast	Kuste	côte	costa
beach	Strand	la plage	playa
ebb tide	Ebbe	reflux	bajamar
flood tide	Flut	flux	pleamar
incoming tide	auflaufend	marée montante	marea arriba
outgoing tide	ablaufend	marée descendante	marea abajo
sandbank	Sandbank	banc de sable	banco de arena
reef	Riff	brisant	arrecife
waves	Wellen	vagues	olas
swell	Dunung	houle	mar de fondo
surf	Brandung	déferlantes	rompiente, surf
sky	Himmel	ciel	cielo

WEATHER	WETTER	LE TEMPS	EL TIEMPO
temperature	temperatur	température	temperatura
warm	warm	chaud	calido
cold	kalt	froid	fresco
mild	mild	clément	moderado
sun	Sonne	soleil	sol
sunny	heiter	ensoleillé	despejado
clouds	Wolken	nuages	nubes
cloudy	wolkig	nuageux	nuboso
rain	Regen	pluie	lluvia
shower	Schauer	averse	chubasco
thunderstorm	Gewitter	orage	tormenta
thermal	Thermik	brise thermique	termico
warm front	Warmfront	front chaud	frente calido
cold front	Kaltfront	front froid	frente frio
high pressure	Hochdruckgebiet	anticyclone	alta presion
low pressure	Tiefdruckgebiet	dépression	baja presion

WIND	WIND	VENT	VIENTO
light	schwach	faible	flojo
moderate	maBig	modéré	moderado
strong	stark	fort	fuerte
increasing	zunehmend	forcissant	aumentando
decreasing	abflauend	faiblissant	disminuyendo
shifting	drehend	tournant	cambiando
offshore	ablandig	de terre	de tierra
onshore	auflandig	de mer	del mar
storm	Sturm	tempête	temporal
stormy	sturmisch	tempétueux	tempestuoso
gusty	boig	en rafales	racheado
gale warning	Sturmwarnung	avis de tempête	aviso de tormenta
hurricane	Orkan	ouragan	huracan

2   THE BEAUFORT SCALE

The Beaufort scale is an easy reference for sailors wishing to know the force of the wind. Ideal conditions for shortboard sailing exist between force 5 to 7. Stronger winds can be survived or even revelled in but are for advanced sailors only. Lighter breezes require large sails and voluminous boards.

BEAUFORT	KM/HR	M/S	KNOTS	DESCRIPTION
0	<1	<0.2	<1	calm
1	1–5	0.3–1.5	1–3	smoke begins to blow
2	6–11	1.6–3.3	4–6	light breeze
3	12–19	3.4–5.4	7–10	gentle breeze
4	20–28	5.5–7.9	11–15	moderate breeze
5	29–38	8.0–10.7	16–21	fresh breeze
6	39–49	10.8–13.8	22–27	strong breeze
7	50–61	13.9–17.1	28–33	near gale
8	62–74	17.2–20.7	34–40	gale
9	75–88	20.8–24.4	41–47	severe gale
10	89–102	24.5–28.4	48–55	very severe gale
11	103–117	28.5–32.6	56–63	verging on hurricane
12	>117	>32.6	>63	hurricane

Index